Tim Carey's new book, *Control in the Classroom,* is a great addition to the educational literature. It introduces educators to the most important and revolutionary new development in psychology in decades, Perceptual Control Theory. And it does this in an easy, accessible style. It has something for everyone in education, from pre-school teachers to secondary teachers, as well as their students. Even college instructors and educational policy makers can find much of value in this slim volume. (Don't be put off by the drawings and light-hearted presentation.)

Carey points out that all of us, not only teachers and students, are structured to try to control our own perceptions of what we want to see. We do this through acting in our environment to bring our perceptions in line with what Carey calls our "just-rights", our desires and goals. In other words, behavior is the control of perceptions.

And, of course, when someone is acting to control his or her perceptions, other people are often also in the environment, trying to control their perceptions in terms of their "just-rights." These other folks efforts at controlling their perceptions means that their actions may help one's' efforts to control, may be a disturbance and be resisted, or may not affect one's' efforts at control. Carey insightfully explores these features of perceptual control theory for the interactions of students and schools, students and teachers, students and testers, teachers and schools. In the end, his advice is that we educators should "structure the environment such that everyone has the opportunity to control their own experiences with a minimum of interference."

Read this book! You'll be glad you did.

Hugh G. Petrie, Ph.D.
Professor Emeritus and former Dean,
Graduate School of Education
State University of New York at Buffalo

Control in the Classroom

an adventure in learning and achievement

Timothy A. Carey

Living Control Systems Publishing
Menlo Park, CAA

Copyright © 2012 by Timothy A. Carey

All rights reserved.

Cover art by Margaret and Jack Carey.
Illustrations by Jack Carey (age 5).

Library of Congress Control Number: 2012941573

Publishers Cataloging in Publication
    Carey, Timothy Andrew, 1963 –
    Control in the classroom :
       an adventure in learning and achievement.
    xxiii, 155 p. : illustrated : 24 cm.

       978-1-938090-10-3   (softcover, perfect binding)
       978-1-938090-11-0   (hardcover, case binding)

       1. Control 2. Psychology 3. Perceptual Control Theory
       4. Effective Teaching 5. Motivation in Education
       6. Learning 7. Classroom Management

    I. Title.

LB 3013.C   2012

♾ The paper used in this book meets all ANSI standards for archival quality paper.

Margaret and Jack – for you, because of you, with you

This book

Control in the Classroom
An Adventure in Learning and Achievement

is available as a free PDF download from the publisher's website, www.livingcontrolsystems.com, as well as the free online libraries www.archive.org and www.z-lib.org, which will help ensure that this book and others on the subject of *Perceptual Control Theory, PCT,* will be available to students for many decades to come.

File name: ControlClassroomCarey2012.pdf

The file is password protected. Changes are not allowed. Printing at high resolution and content copying are allowed. Before you print, check the modest price from your favorite Internet bookstore.

For related books and papers, search *Perceptual Control Theory*

For drop ship volume orders, mix and match, contact the publisher.

contents

About this Book	ix
Acknowledgements	xi
Foreword	xv
Preamble	xix
About the Forms	xxiii
1: How Do You Do?	1
2: Much Ado About Nothing?	13
3: Learning From a Control Perspective	21
4: Tying Up a Few Loose Ends	37
5: Giving Schools a PCA Revamp	49
6: Setting the Scene in the Classroom	69
7: Going About the Business of Teaching	87
8: Assessment in Educational Settings	111
9: Classroom Procedures	123
Useful Websites	135
Recommended Reading	137
Blank Forms	145

about this book

Have you ever wondered how learning happens? *Control in the Classroom* introduces the main ideas of a profound explanation of human behavior and then applies these ideas to the issue of curriculum delivery. This illuminating explanation, known as Perceptual Control Theory, shows that control is the fundamental phenomenon at the core of the business of living. Control is critical in the classroom – both for teachers and for students.

From this perspective, teaching can be considered to be a process of helping students develop greater control capabilities. The first part of the book introduces the theory in an easy-to-read, light-hearted style. Through an abundance of examples the principles of the theory are applied both to classroom activity and life in general. You might even discover that understanding this theory helps you in other areas of your life, not only in teaching. The second part of the book addresses specific aspects of curriculum delivery such as lesson plans and goal setting. Forms are provided to help you develop expertise in this approach. Examples of completed forms are included as well.

This exciting and intriguing book will be an invaluable resource for both inexperienced and seasoned teachers. Any educator who wants to improve life in the classroom by taking a behind-the-scenes peek at what might be going on when students learn will be delighted with this book. By taking some time to understand the important principles and becoming familiar with the suggested forms and practices, teachers will be able to help themselves and their students have more rewarding experiences in the classroom. With this book in your collection, walking into your classroom really will be embarking on an adventure in learning and achievement.

acknowledgements

Many of the ideas in this book first began to sprout in the enthralling conversations I've been fortunate to have with a raft of different people. I've had the very good fortune to spend time with talented educators, scientists, clinicians, and theoreticians who have provided different perspectives and learnings for which I've been grateful.

In terms of Perceptual Control Theory (PCT), I've learned from the very best. My attention and application might not always have been as diligent as it should have been but the teachers were of the highest caliber. Bill Powers, Tom Bourbon, and Rick Marken were instrumental. So too were Phil Runkel and Mary Powers. My experience of the world is all the richer for having mixed with these friends.

A number of astute and enthusiastic educators provided valuable guidance as I was finalising the text. I benefitted from the advice of Damian Nelson, Peter Marcon, Grace Gadsby, Jean Knight, Glenn Vaughan, Judy and Jenny McFadden, Fred and Perry Good, Lloyd Klinedinst, Thea and Ed Vanags, Heather Pedrotti, Janette Jacob, John Kirkland, and June Myatt. Perspectives outside education were also extremely helpful and Richard Mullan, Chris and Margaret Spratt, Sara Tai, and Warren Mansell who are good friends and remarkable clinicians have spent time understanding the concepts and helping me achieve greater clarity and relevance in my explanations. In the late '90s I spent time working with Ed Ford and learned many things from him.

As publication drew nearer Bruce Nevin's editorial suggestions helped improve the readability of the book and Dag Forssell carried out his publisher role in the meticulous way that ensures high quality. Bruce and Dag both have advanced understandings of PCT which made their contributions all the more valuable. I was delighted that Jo Earp, the Editor of *Australian Teacher Magazine*, agreed to write the foreword for the book.

The children I've been privileged to teach over the years have had a powerful influence on me and helped me arrive at my current thinking on the various topics I cover in this book. I hope I was a useful teacher – I know I was a grateful student.

It is especially exciting for me that Margaret and Jack were able to contribute to this book by providing the artwork for the cover and the chapter pages (as well as Margaret's tireless proof reading and discussing of the concepts. As a teacher, psychologist, and keen PCTer she is a sounding board like no other). Thanks, you two, for everything you are – and everything I am when I'm with you. Life is good when you're around.

foreword

I was thrilled when Tim asked me to write the foreword for his new book.

As an editor, I've thoroughly enjoyed reading his monthly Tim's Tales articles for *Australian Teacher Magazine*.

As a former primary teacher I've wished on more than one occasion in the last two-and-a-half years that his advice and observations had been available to me during my stint in the classroom.

Funnily enough, when he said the book was called *Control in the Classroom* I was transported back to my days working in the kind of UK inner city schools that often get labelled 'challenging' by government inspectors.

But, rather than being a book about behavior management it's a fascinating take on what may be going on inside the heads of your students … well, actually, inside all our heads.

Instead of passing judgement on your school and classroom environment, it introduces you to Perceptual Control Theory and its approach to curriculum planning and delivery, then gives useful examples for how it might help transform your own teaching practice.

Without giving too much away, before you know it you'll be chatting to colleagues about PCAs, Lego bricks of the mind, catapults and launching missions to hunt for controlled variables so you can gently disturb "just-rights" and help your students groove.

One of the great things I've noticed about Tim's magazine columns is the way he offers up a thoroughly informative academic perspective on a particular issue, all the while maintaining an easy-to-read and often light-hearted style.

He also has a wonderful ability to draw you in as a reader by making you feel like you're listening to a personal friend, and *Control in the Classroom* is no different.

Jo Earp
Editor, Australian Teacher Magazine
Melbourne, June 2012

preamble

When I worked as a behavior management teacher I used to help classroom teachers think about ways to work more effectively with students having behavioral difficulties. Back then I always got the feeling that something was missing. I worked with individual teachers and individual students, with class groups, and with whole schools, and the focus of our work was always to change one undesirable behavior or another. Many of these behaviors are disruptive to a greater or lesser extent and so the argument has always been that if we could just sort out these behaviors then teachers would be able to get on with their job of teaching. It's a convincing rationale but it also seems a bit paralyzing in certain respects because teachers can't get on with the business of teaching, or at least not get on with it as they would like to, until this behavior business is sorted out.

Along the way I discovered a quite unusual explanation of behavior called Perceptual Control Theory (PCT). PCT is what this whole book is about, so I won't give too much away just yet. It's enough to say, though, that learning about this theory gave me a new understanding of behavior and a new appreciation of what to expect in schools.

Considering things the PCT way helped me to see that there will *always* be behaviors in *any* school that one or more people find objectionable. We are *never* going to get to the point in any school where everyone is behaving "desirably" all the time.

Striving for that is like searching for that pot of gold at the end of the rainbow...

Rather than being depressing, I found that realization liberating. If we take for granted that, at any particular time, some people in a social group will behave in ways that others in the group find disconcerting, we can start from there and think about the situation differently. We know behavior problems exist in schools. They always have, they always will. My suggestion is that we build a big bridge and get over it. Let's see how good schools can be if we just assume that children's behavior during the day will range from extremely annoying to delightfully charming depending on what's happening and whose point of view we adopt.

At this point, let me make clear that I'm not wanting to denigrate or dismiss the many valuable and worthwhile approaches that work on ways of helping people in schools get along better. There's a plethora of material out there of varying levels of usefulness (within that plethora I find anything based on PCT to be particularly useful) and I think there's a place for all of it. We never know what material is going to strike a chord with which teacher.

What there doesn't seem to be so much of is an application of theories of behavior to the core business of curriculum delivery. That's where this book comes in. I suppose I'm putting the cart back behind the horse and saying – *Let's suppose behavior in schools is as good now as it's ever going to be. Can we start from here and see how far we can go with learning and achievement if we apply to curriculum delivery issues the same resourcefulness we allocate to behavior problems.*

That's what this book is about. It may very well fit alongside a lot of the classroom management books you might already have acquired. It will snuggle in most comfortably with books based on PCT because that's what this book is based upon.

This book is a PCT approach to curriculum delivery starting with a PCT understanding of what happens when we learn.

I can't put it more clearly than that, so if your interest is piqued, let's get started…

about the forms

Throughout the book I've provided some forms that might be useful for developing your teaching along the lines of what I describe. The examples used in the "Why?" and "How?" sheets are Achievement Standards taken from the Australian national curriculum, www.australiancurriculum.edu.au. Examples from different grades (2, 4, 8, and 10) and subject areas (English, Science, Mathematics, and History) are used.

These examples are provided as possibilities of different ways the sheets can be completed. They don't necessarily represent the right way or the only way to complete the forms. I'm hoping that these examples of completed forms might help to further explain some of the concepts I'm outlining.

With your knowledge of your students and their capabilities, you will probably have different responses from the ones I've provided. That is as it should be. In fact, once you've got a handle on the concepts I'm explaining I would be delighted to learn that you'd used the underlying principles to generate your own forms. The ideas I present here are intended to be a beginning rather than the definitive answer.

How Do You Do?

*If you read this chapter
you'll learn how
people go about
doing things
— anything!*

How Do You Do?

Let's face it – teachers teach people how to do things. Or, to say it another way, people learn how to do things from teachers. People learn how to color in without going over the lines, or how to structure a scientific report, or how to say "More bread please" in French, or how to share six apples equally among three people, or how to hit a topspin lob, or how to knit one pearl one, or how to play Mozart's Minuet in G Minor, or how to spell "supercalifragilisticexpialidocious".

When you consider the number of things a person learns by the time they become an adult, it's easy to appreciate the tremendously important job that teachers have. To be sure, not everything a person learns is taught formally to them by a trained teacher. Most people don't have lessons to walk and talk but they still learn to do these things proficiently. Despite these obvious examples, it is still the case that, of all the things a person can do, a great number of these doings were taught to them by teachers.

If teachers teach people how to do things, it makes sense to start a book for teachers with an explanation about how people do things. And if a book such as this is to appeal to a wide range of teachers, the explanation should be general enough to cover a multitude of doings. An explanation of how people save money and build share portfolios would be useful to a financial manager but perhaps of little interest to a year 9 geography teacher. Fortunately, although there is great variability in *what* people do, it turns out that if we look at things in a particular way, *how* people do things is remarkably similar. Whether it's different people doing different things – perhaps one person is traveling to Peru and the other person is learning their spelling list – or whether it's the same person doing different things – perhaps at 7.37 am Briony is packing her lunch and at 2.37 pm she is providing the summary for her debating team – there's a way to look behind these differences and find a common process occurring.

It's important to understand and recognize this process if we're to take a giant leap forward in the way we help people learn. For the most part, teachers have been doing a great job helping people learn without knowing about this process. I think we could scale loftier heights if we knew about this process and used it to guide our teaching.

Good teachers may implicitly already know about this process. They could become even better at teaching by focusing on it explicitly. Teachers who don't have the success of their more adept colleagues could find understanding this process a huge help by providing guidance and structure to what they do.

The idea is that this process is the process of doing, so if you know the process you'll be in a good position to help people learn to do things.

So, after that literary drum roll, it might be mundanely surprising to know that the process is just the process of making things happen repeatedly. Although I said this was mundane, I didn't really mean that. It's actually one of Nature's most amazing accomplishments. It's right up there with magnetism, lightning, and gravity. People (and all other living creatures as it turns out) can make things happen time and time again even though the conditions under which they produce these happenings are almost never the same twice.

People drive themselves to work even though the traffic on the road is never the same two days in a row. People create lasting friendships even though friends grow up, get married, and move away. People maintain a sense of "Who I am" even though they go on self-improvement courses, get degrees, and see someone in the mirror they don't always recognize. People shoot three pointers over and over again even though it's at a different stage of the game, the score is different, they're in a different place at the top of the key, in a different stadium, with different opponents, and their energy level is different.

The process underlying all these things is called control. Control, in this sense, pretty much means just what you think it might mean. To control something means to make it do what you want. If you control your dog when you take it for a walk that means it walks where you want when you want. If you control the temperature of the lounge room that means you adjust the thermostat (or open the window) so that it feels the way you want.

It turns out that life is about control ... in a sense, we are all control freaks so you don't have to worry about anyone accusing you of that anymore! At a very basic level, if we didn't control things like the amount of food we eat and how warm we feel, we'd die. Controlling the way things are is essential to our very existence. This stuff really is about life and death – it's that important! Think about how far down the road you'd get if you weren't able to control the position and speed of your car. The reason that speeding, drunk driving, and going to sleep at the wheel are so dangerous is because they interfere with our ability to control the car.

The road of life is much like the road of asphalt. We have a far better time on the road if we're able to control the things that are important to us. Teaching is about helping people learn to control things. When people learn to do long division they learn to control a little program in their heads so that they can make the same steps happen over and over again even though the numbers might be different every time. When people learn to sing in harmony they learn to control the pitch and timing of their voice even though where they're singing, and what they're singing, and who they're singing with, can all be different.

Teaching, then, is about control. Understanding how people do what they do is about understanding how people control. Luckily, that's not so difficult. If we step back into the lounge room we can think about how we go about controlling the temperature there. There are three things we need to know. Firstly, we have to be able to tell what the temperature is – maybe we can feel it, or maybe we can see a number that tells us what it is. We also have to know if the current temperature is too hot, too cold, or just right. (Have you ever been in a room that you thought was too cold but someone else thought was just right?) And we have to be able to do something to change too hot or too cold to just right.

I have more to say about "just-rights" later because they play a big role in understanding behavior and helping people learn. I've discovered that my wife and I have different just-rights for the distance between our car and the one in front. My just-right is much smaller than my wife's so, when I'm driving, she's constantly applying an imaginary brake on the passenger side and, when she's driving, I can't understand why we're going so slowly and hanging so far back from the rest of the traffic!

For someone to control the state of the answer sheet they submit at the end of a multiple-choice exam they have to be able to read the questions and the responses. They have to be able to compare the responses they see with what they think is the correct response and they have to have some way of marking the form to indicate which item on the form matches the idea they have in their head.

No matter what the activity is, if it's a control process – if pretty much the same outcomes are happening despite changing conditions and circumstances – it always involves perceiving, comparing, and acting. You can't control the sweetness of your coffee if you can't taste the coffee, compare it to how sweet you like it to be, and do something if it is too sweet or too bitter in order to make it be just right. Note that you don't need to be able to perceive, compare, and act in order to be able to change something. You could change the sweetness of your coffee just by pouring in the entire sugar bowl. Changing something, however, is not the same as controlling something. To control is to change something *systematically*.

So perceiving, comparing, and acting are what we do to control things. To control the noise level in his classroom, Mr. Hardacre has to be able to hear the current noise level, compare it to the noise level he prefers, and act in order to make what he's hearing match his preference. This example also serves to illustrate that, sometimes, our preferences change. When it's time for science or art Mr. Hardacre might prefer a noise level that is different from the level he prefers when it's silent reading time. Whatever his preference at any particular point in time, control works just the same. He'll compare what he is hearing with what he wants to hear and act to make "is" and "wants" be the same.

Perceiving, comparing, and acting share a special relationship. They are all going on all the time and affecting each other simultaneously. As the noise level in Mr. Hardacre's class begins to rise he will start to do things to make it just right again. He won't wait until it reaches maximum volume before he compares it to his internal standard. (If "internal standard" sounds too stuffy to you call it a "goal" or an "expectation" or a "want" or some other term you prefer that indicates the desired state of affairs.) This simultaneity makes it completely arbitrary to separate cause and effect. The change in noise level effects Mr. Hardacre's behavior and Mr. Hardacre's behavior affects the noise level. Cause-effect rules take on a different kind of meaning for living things because they control.

If you're interested in reading some more about the way in which we perceive, compare, and act, it's fortunate that there is a growing literature on that topic. I mentioned that the formal explanation for this process is called Perceptual Control Theory (PCT). This was developed by William T. Powers (Bill). You would do well to read anything of Bill's that you can get your hands on. Many other people have spent a great deal of time, energy, and enthusiasm learning about Bill's work and have created numerous publications to complement Bill's own writings. At the back of this book, I've provided a smattering of the ones I think you might find useful or interesting or both, along with websites that might be helpful.

Now, back to control. The "how" of control is explained by the presence of a little perceiving-comparing-acting (PCA) unit for everything we control. That might sound like a lot of units but if you think of the gazillions of neurons we have at our disposal it's not asking too much really. So, essentially, what we are is a myriad of PCAs connected hierarchically and in parallel. Some PCAs – like the ones controlling love and happiness – tell other PCAs – like the ones controlling work and play – what their current standard is. In the example above, Mr. Hardacre's PCA for task engagement varied the volume for his PCA of noise level depending on the task at hand.

Growing, developing, and learning, then, is a bit like building with Lego. It's a matter of putting little PCAs together and then fitting them into, on top of, beside, behind, underneath, and in front of PCAs that are already there. When new PCAs are added or grown they need time to bed down into their appropriate place in the network. Once the PCA has nestled in, the entire system (which is a pretty cold way of describing a student in your class! But don't despair – this description applies to you too!) will have abilities that it didn't have before. Developing and connecting PCAs and then fitting them into the entire PCA network might be an interesting way to start thinking about learning. By implication then, the job of a teacher is to help this happen.

From this perspective, one of the most interesting aspects of the job of teaching is that we can't directly adjust, manipulate, or construct the PCAs we need to affect. Whereas sculptors chisel, chip, or mold the actual material they work with, teachers never have that luxury. In that sense, it's not exactly like building with Lego, or at least, it's a Lego building you can't actually put together yourself.

PCA units exist inside the head of each person. We can get a sense of the PCAs any particular individual has by the way in which they interact with their environment, but we can't deal with these PCAs directly. Not ever. This makes teaching a very tricky business. Successfully teaching someone something means that a little PCA or a group of PCAs is created and becomes well practiced and efficient. Teachers can play a big part in this creation but, ultimately, it's the learner or student who has to put the PCA together.

While I sincerely hope that lots of teachers love this book and are inspired by it, I'd like to think that students will be the main beneficiaries. Clever students seem to be able to learn in almost any situation. Sometimes, students even seem to learn in spite of their teachers rather than because of them. Students who are not so clever, however, can find school a pretty daunting and formidable place. If we can lift the lid on this process of learning, and begin to understand what's involved at the most basic level, perhaps schools will become places where all students can experience a greater degree of success.

Looking under the hood might take some of the mystery out of learning but I hope that doesn't make the process any less beautiful, magical, or amazing. For me, knowing what's involved in learning has made it even more wonderful than it was before. Discovering that Michelangelo's statue of David emerged from a block of marble didn't make David any less stunning or captivating to me. I guess you could say that Michelangelo discovered the David that was hidden in the marble. In the same way, when we know what we're working with, I hope teachers will be able to encourage the talents of all students to emerge and shine through. Think of this book as a manual for being educationally useful to students. I have this tingling little feeling that, by understanding learning this way, we might be able to add wings to the feet of our students and help them soar to places they didn't think were possible. Perhaps we'll eventually have to start calling teachers "catapulters" because of the effect they have on the learning and achievement of their students by understanding the process of control.

So there you have it. Teachers help people put together PCAs. You could think of good teaching as "Lego of the mind"! Understanding this hands-off approach to Lego construction and doing it effectively and efficiently is what this book is all about. Throughout the book I focus on what might need to happen to help students develop the PCAs that are required. Along the way, I hope you will also find that your own PCAs with respect to teaching are enriched and enhanced.

How Do You Do?

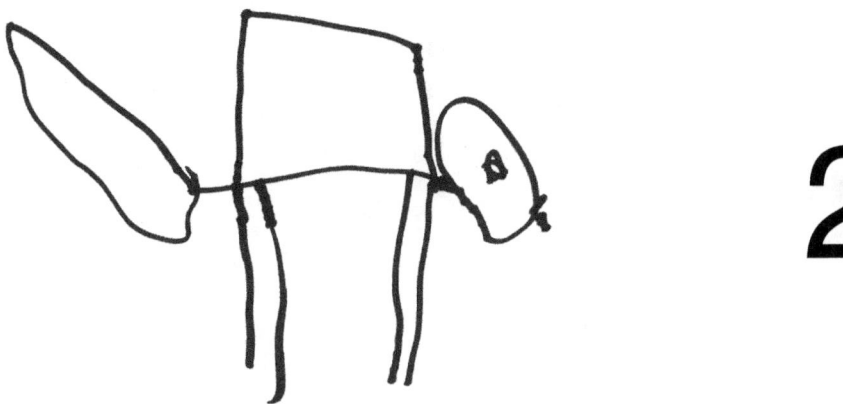

Much Ado About Nothing?

*If you read this chapter
you'll find out why
this book will become
your next best friend!*

Much Ado About Nothing?

In the previous chapter I gave some indication as to why I think a book like this might be important. I want to expand on those ideas in this chapter. Given the voluminous stockpile of books that exist about teaching and learning I wouldn't blame you if you were just a little skeptical about another book promising something new. Well, this time is different! I bet you've heard that before too.

It's not uncommon among teachers to hear the view that trends in education seem to occur in cycles. If you stick around long enough you'll see things become the flavor of the month, then become unfashionably distasteful, and then come back into vogue again. In that sense, "revolution" is a very appropriate way of describing many innovations in education. Pretty soon we revolve right back to where we were before. "Coming full circle" is perhaps another way of describing the same thing.

Thinking of learning in terms of PCAs offers a new opportunity. With this conceptualization in mind it's possible to set off on a quite different path in education. Sometimes though, the differences won't be superficially obvious. That's because the change will have occurred at a much more fundamental level. Way back when we weren't as clever as we are now, we used to believe that the earth was the center of the universe and that the sun traveled across our sky, rising in the east and setting in the west. As we became wiser, we discovered that, actually, the reverse is happening. The sun is at the center (perhaps not the center of the universe, but it's at the center of what matters to us) and the phenomenon of the sun appearing in the east and disappearing in the west occurs because of the rotation of the earth. Even with this knowledge we still call these phenomena "sunrises" and "sunsets" and we still find them incredibly beautiful. Somehow it just wouldn't be as romantic to say "Honey, let's grab a bottle of wine and go down to the beach to watch the earth rotate a little bit", but we still know what's going on.

Similarly, there was a time when people believed that the world was flat. In that time, when they observed ships sailing over the horizon, it was only natural to suppose that they were falling off the earth. Later, however, when we realized that the world was a globe we could rest easily when those ships disappeared from view. Importantly, however, *we still observe the same thing*. We still see ships sail out to sea and disappear over the edge of the horizon. Changing our knowledge of the shape of the earth didn't change our observations – it changed our understanding of what was happening. And with this new understanding, people of that time were able to set sail with confidence, traveling into the unknown, having adventures, and making discoveries that wouldn't have been possible before.

So it could be with a PCA approach to schooling. I don't want to appear critical or dismissive of the many advances that have been made so far but (you knew there was going to be a "but" didn't you?), in many ways, we're still a flat earth when it comes to schools. Thinking of learning from a PCA perspective (the Perceive-Compare-Act cycle) won't necessarily change what you observe on a day-to-day basis in your classrooms. It *will* change, however, how you understand your observations. Because you will understand your observations differently you'll be able to take different courses of action that will reap greater rewards for you and your students. PCAing offers a new adventure in learning and achievement for educators in schools.

I could let you in on a little secret and tell you that I think this PCA approach to education has the potential to fundamentally and resolutely transform the way we think about schools and the business that goes on there. I think we could see much greater learning and achievement with students and many more satisfied teachers. One day, in a distant and sunnier time, it might be quite commonplace for a parent to ask at the dinner table "So Francine, how many PCAs did you build in school today?". In my wildest dreams, late at night, I imagine this book becoming an international bestseller, translated into different languages, and fame and untold wealth showering down upon me …

My immediate goals, however, are a little more humble (I dabble in humility from time to time). I like to think there'll be something in this book for just about any teacher. Teachers in my experience are a pretty resilient and creative bunch. They're used to making the best out of not very much and they're experts at finding ways to succeed in less than ideal conditions. This book might help with some unobtrusive ways of making these tasks easier.

The only teachers this book might not have something for are those teachers who are as successful as they want to be all of the time. There may be some of these kinds of teachers in existence but I've never met them. If you are one of those teachers then I should warn you that if you continue to read the book, you might not get that much out of it.

I've written this book for those teachers who would like to be more successful at curriculum planning and delivery than they are now. This isn't so much a book about classroom management. It's a book that could accompany texts about management practices. If you've ever had a class who weren't as engaged with the material you were teaching as you'd like them to be, or if you've ever taught a lesson that sailed right over the students' heads, or if there's a student who stands out in your memory that you just weren't able to get through to as much as you'd like, or students who you maybe thought could have been achieving much more than they were, then this book might have something for you.

Perhaps there's a particular lesson or topic that, year after year, you've found hard to teach to students so that they understand it comprehensively. This book might give you some ideas for how to "unpack" the concepts in ways that match the students' capabilities. You'll be able to plan lessons and units of work with an understanding of what will be happening for the students when they take meaning from your efforts. This is a book about teaching from the perspective of the learner. It's a book from the inside looking out, if you like. If we start with that perspective we might be able to figure out ways of helping outside information go in more efficiently and effectively.

If you've never encountered recurrent difficulties with particular teaching content, has there ever been a student who didn't seem to learn despite your best efforts? With the ideas in this book you'll be able to consider them and their situation differently. You might be able to peek beneath the surface and make some informed guesses about the way the machinery is working. With these guesses you'll have a better sense of what to do next. This book won't necessarily provide answers for every tricky situation you're likely to encounter in a classroom but it might give you a systematic, thorough, and effective way of figuring out your own best answers for your particular circumstances.

Even teachers of students who have been labeled or diagnosed with particular learning disorders could benefit from the ideas in this book. The PCA approach to learning and achievement offers a fresh way of understanding where the problems might be when learning doesn't occur as easily as it might. That doesn't mean you'll be putting "A$^+$s" on every student's report card but it might mean that students are able to get more out of their own talents and strengths and personal styles than they do at the moment.

Teachers of very young children as well as teachers of much older children should find something of value in this book. Because I'm focusing on the process of learning, these ideas are applicable whether you're learning colors or calculus. My very bold proposal is that, whatever the concepts being learned, a similar process of constructing PCAs is going on. Sometimes more PCAs might need to be built, or more existing PCAs might be affected by the new PCA in the neighborhood but the same process is still involved.

So, I hope by this stage you'll agree that there is much 'adoing' to be made about a different direction in our current approach to teaching in schools. It's true that schools currently do a fine job for a lot of students a lot of the time. For some students, however, we miss the mark big time and, when this occurs, we seem unable to step back and think about things differently. We might make things simpler or give more focused attention but we still approach learning and achievement in the same way. When things don't proceed as they should, however, it might help to have a closer look at how things work. I've written this book to help lift the lid on the process of learning from the perspective of the learner.

For the great majority of the time, people don't need to think about what's going on under the hood of their car. They just jump in, turn the key, and set off. Sometimes, however, the car won't start or won't travel as smoothly as it did before. When that happens, someone needs to find out what's going on in the workings of the car. I've taken the same approach in this book. I very much subscribe to the "if it ain't broke don't fix it" method. For those students, classes, and lessons where things are happening as you'd like them to, continue doing what you're doing. When you encounter situations, however, where the plan doesn't unfold in the way that you thought it might, it could be helpful to think about what's going on. This book is a way of helping you do that. Keep it close by. When you find yourself grinding your teeth in frustration or feeling as though you're hitting your head against a brick wall or just not being as amazing as you'd like to be, it might be your best friend.

20

3

Learning From a Control Perspective

*If you read this chapter
you'll find out about
the important elements to
building networks of PCAs*

Learning From a Control Perspective

If it really is the case (and there's some pretty good evidence to suggest it is) that what we call learning is the construction or reconfiguring of PCAs, then, when people learn, they must learn to perceive, compare, and act with respect to the subject matter they're mastering. When young children learn to reach out and grab things they must learn to perceive, compare, and act with regard to the experience of seeing and feeling their hand wrap around an object that has caught their attention. When people learn to play the piano they must learn to perceive, compare, and act with regard to hearing a particular combination of notes occur in a particular way. The same thing applies when someone learns a second language or how to differentiate and integrate.

When someone learns to drive a car they learn to create and then maintain a particular speed of the car and a particular position of the car on the road and a particular distance behind the car in front. When people learn to walk they learn to maintain their body position in a particular posture and move it around their environment. Have you ever noticed the way someone changes the way they lean if they walk up a hill or down a hill. They don't have to be told to do this, they just do it. Such is the wonder of control with PCAs – once they're in place, they look after all the tedious details for you. So, once you've established the particular orientation to the ground that you'd prefer (let's call it "vertical"!), the PCA will make sure that happens regardless (across some pretty broad changes in scenery) of the lay of the land.

The same applies for pianists when they learn to create particular sounds. Pianists learn to perceive the position and movement of their fingers on the keyboard in relation to the sounds that they hear. They learn to compare the sounds they are producing with the sounds they intend to produce and they learn to act in order to make what they are hearing match what they want to hear. Through good teaching they put together a PCA that can cope with different contexts and settings.

The same process occurs whether the learning involves riding a bike or baking a cake or writing a novel or any other activity. People take art classes because they cannot create the strokes on a canvas that they have imagined in their mind's eye. People take tennis lessons because they cannot make the tennis ball do what they want it to do. People hire math tutors because they cannot manipulate symbols as precisely as they would like to. The extent to which the art teacher or the tennis coach or the math tutor is helpful will depend on the extent to which they are able to help the individual in each case construct a PCA which allows them to make things happen the way they want. The result of good teaching is that learners achieve greater control of something: greater control of the production of visual images, greater control of the movement of the tennis ball, greater control of the manipulation of math symbols, and so on. Greater control from their perspective that is.

This approach to learning – helping people construct PCAs – raises some very helpful questions for teachers.

Is Jim able to notice (or perceive) what he is learning to control?

If Jim has a severe hearing impairment he will have difficulty learning to produce the sounds of speech because he cannot hear the sounds he is making. If Lauren has an extensive visual impairment she will not learn to discriminate colors the way sighted people do because she is not able to sense different colors visually. In order to control something we first have to be able to notice or detect that particular thing. Have you noticed the way that food loses its flavor when you have a cold? Imagine if you were like that permanently – it would be very difficult to create culinary masterpieces with the right blend of secret herbs and spices if you couldn't taste the brew you had mixed. If Jim has a visual impairment, even if it is less severe than Lauren's, he may not be able to see the chalkboard clearly from where he is sitting. Sometimes, the first step in helping people learn is just making sure they can notice or detect the thing they are trying to control. Perhaps there is some specific and important detail they're missing because they're looking at the big picture. People who are very expert at something can forget the particular things that are important to pay attention to at the novice stage. In order to know what to point out to a learner, it might help to devote some thought to all the necessary elements of a task.

When problems occur, figuring out what people see or recognize can be helpful. Some people have trouble reading or calculating, for example, because they do not see written symbols the way many other people see them. Similarly, if we're interested in students controlling things like respect and cooperation it's good to find out what they know about these things. Would they recognize respect if it showed up in front of them? Would they know when someone was cooperating with them?

Can Sophia remember what she has perceived?

If Sophia is to learn to control the amount of meaning she derives from printed matter she will need to be able to remember what letters look like. She will need to be able to differentiate letters from nonletters. If she wants to control the correctness of a mathematical solution she will need to be able to remember the sequence of steps involved in solving the problem. She will also need to be able to remember acceptable steps from steps that are not permissible. Prompts, guides, and cue cards can be very useful for students when they are learning something that requires them to remember a sequence of steps or some important symbols.

Issues like these can be important to keep in mind in situations such as testing (I have more to say about testing and assessment later in the book). When we're testing students, and when we're considering the results of testing, one factor that might help make sense of some of the results is the extent to which students are able to retain the concepts that are being tested. If you have some doubts about their memory have a quick check about other tasks at school. Do they remember your name and their friends' names? Do they remember where their desk is? Do they remember when it's time for lunch? If you offer them a treat (just something they like) after a particular activity, do they remember the deal you made? Answers to these questions will give you some sense of the capabilities of their memory. Sometimes the machinery is working appropriately but what we're asking them to learn is so different from all the other PCAs they currently have that the new PCA has trouble fitting in. Finding out about the student and the ways in which they understand their world can often give you some clues about where a new PCA might fit best.

Does Ben have a preferred state of what he is controlling?

The idea of a preferred state of something is a crucial aspect of the whole PCA game. The preferred state is important during the comparison phase. In the morning before work when you're looking in the mirror, you're comparing what you see reflected back at you with what you want to see. When your hair is just right (or right enough) and your outfit is just right (or all you have time for at the moment) you'll set off for work (or at least move away from the mirror). I mentioned just-rights before and said they were important. The just-rights are the things that tell the PCAs what the current standard or goal is. Essentially, the just-right says to its PCA "make it be *this* way". The just-rights cover all that we do – make my relationship be this way, make my coffee be this way, make the speed of my car be this way, make the report I'm writing be this way, and so on.

A young child, for example, might know that the letters "d", "g", and "o" can be connected in a just-right way to create a written representation for their favorite pet. If they want to communicate their ideas effectively with other people they need to establish a standard of "d-o-g" when they connect these letters. Other combinations like "d-g-o" or "o-g-d" or g-d-o" just won't cut it. If Ben has trouble spelling "dog" one way of checking whether he has established the appropriate standard or not would be to put all the different combinations on different cards. You could show him a picture of a pooch and ask him to pick out the card that tells you what it's a picture of. Can he do it? If not, maybe he needs more practice at establishing the appropriate standard for the way the letters are combined. Spelling provides a clear example of the idea of a standard or benchmark for variable combinations of letters. Imagine all the ways that the letters "supercalifragilisticexpialidocious" might be combined. There is only one combination of these letters, however, that will be correct if you want to sing along with Mary Poppins.

When I first began communicating over the internet via email I noticed a particular configuration of symbols that regularly appeared in the printed messages I received from other people. The symbols varied slightly but would often be a colon ":", followed by a dash "-", followed by a bracket ")", so that the whole symbol looked like ":-)". As I was new to the game of internet communication I was unaware of the meaning this symbol had and I was puzzled as to why so many people kept making the same peculiar typographical error. It was only one day in casual conversation with an internet veteran that I discovered that the symbol ":-)" was actually ☺ (a "smiley face") on its side. Once I understood what this symbol represented the meaning of a lot of what I read over the internet was different. I now had a benchmark or reference for the symbol.

Is Bianca able to compare her standard or benchmark with the way things currently are?

Essentially, once Bianca has set a just-right state she needs to be able to compare this state with the state she perceives or notices on a moment to moment basis. She needs to be able to tell the difference between what she wants (her just-right) with what she is currently getting. Tom, for example, might regularly misunderstand sarcastic comments. The comments to Tom might not sound different from the comments that he likes to hear. Socially some students may have difficulty telling whether their peers are being nasty or nice. Perhaps this difficulty enables students to be set up in pranks and high-risk activities by peers whose motives are not clear to them. Or perhaps having their peers notice them *is* their just-right. If Sharelle has a just-right for hearing a certain amount of laughter from the other students in the class, this just-right might be more important to her than just-rights about learning and achievement with regard to curriculum material. While this situation remains, Sharelle will do things to achieve the amount of laughter she has specified even if this interferes with her ability to complete set tasks.

An important point to take from this example is that we are always achieving *something*. Our PCAs are always switched on. Sometimes students won't be achieving what you would like them to achieve but that doesn't mean they're not achieving. Figuring out what's going on in terms of what students are achieving at any point in time and gaining some understanding of what PCAs are important to particular students is an important step in knowing what to do next.

Persuasive writing is another example of the importance and relevance of an internal standard or benchmark. When students learn to write persuasively they are learning to control the degree of influence conveyed in their essay. They need, therefore, to be able to compare the degree of influence they would like to communicate with the degree that currently exists in their written work. An inability to compare what you are getting with what you want to get will severely compromise your ability to control.

Is Elizah able to act on the environment in order to change what she is perceiving so that it is like what she intends?

Elizah might know she has got the wrong solution to a math problem but she might not know what to do to correct the problem. Being unhappy with the number of friends you have or the way you are treated by other people does not necessarily mean that you will know how to change that situation. Knowing that you cannot move through water satisfactorily does not automatically imply knowing how to become a more efficient swimmer.

Generally, in order for one PCA to do its job properly, it needs to be able to call upon the services of other PCAs. I mentioned earlier that our PCAs are arranged in parallel and hierarchically to form a large and intricate network. Some PCAs control the same kind of thing and some PCAs control different things. Making sure your car stays the right distance behind the car in front and putting the right flowers beside each other in a flower arrangement might seem like very different things but, in a sense, they're the same *kind* of experience. "Near to" and "beside" are both relationships so these experiences require PCAs that control relationships (not relationships like "friend" or "partner" but spatial relationships like "in front of" and "under"). On the other hand, getting your coffee as hot as you like it and being as honest as you want to be are different kinds of experiences. The coffee experience requires a PCA that controls sensations (you want *this much* hotness) whereas the honesty experience requires a PCA that controls principles or rules (you want *this much* honesty). The hierarchical setup of the network means that the "Ps" at one level combine in different ways to form a more complex "P" at the next level up. That's just a convoluted way of saying that some things we experience are made up of simpler experiences. You can recognize the categories of things like "ball" and "net" without playing a game of tennis but you can't play a game of tennis without some balls and a net. Also, the "As" at one level set the standard for one or more PCAs at the level below. You could think of it like floors in an office building. It's like sending a memo down to the next floor telling them what you want to see on your desk.

Perhaps you have a PCA related to friendship. That PCA might create for you the sense of being a good friend. In order to give you that warm glow inside, the PCA might send a "how often" standard down to the PCA concerned with staying in touch with people. Perhaps the standard is "weekly". The staying in touch with people PCA might use the dialing a telephone PCA to get what it wants. The dialing a telephone PCA will need to use the PCA that distinguishes telephones from televisions and telescopes. This kind of analysis can be continued right down to the PCA that produces the right amount of pressure from your finger to dial the number. And this kind of coordination of PCA upon PCA is involved with all of our activity. Such is the marvel of a hierarchical network of PCAs. It really is wondrous isn't it? You just think "Oh, I'd better give Isaac a call" and the legion of PCAs get to work making it happen. Are you even more impressed now at the amazing job you do when you help people learn?

Even tasks that might seem simple to us require the use of layers and levels of PCAs. For Hannah to control the steps of a math problem, for example, she will need to be able to vary an array of lower level PCAs. Some of the tasks required will be producing the correct sequence of steps of the problem, performing the calculations required at each step, being able to distinguish reliably the categories of "tens" and "units", and being able to produce shapes that look like standard numbers. To control something even more simple such as the shape of a written letter Jack's PCA for correct letter shape will need to use PCAs related to muscle tension in his arm and hand.

Finally, has Eloise had sufficient practice to be able to control this variable smoothly and efficiently under a range of different conditions? You could think about this part as "grooving". When people are learning something new they need to be able to go through the activity over and over. Repeated attempts will groove their PCA connections and iron out the bumps. Have you ever seen a baby when it first reaches for something? Its movements are jerky and unsteady. Over time, however, the babe learns to reach out and grab things sometimes seemingly without even paying attention. I am amazed at how much time a young child will spend doing the same thing over and over again. They seem to know what they need to do to get in the groove. Can you remember your first efforts at driving a manual car? It's difficult at first to coordinate the accelerator and the clutch but gradually, with sufficient time and practice, your efforts become grooved to the point where the driving examiner is satisfied enough to give you your license. Students need sufficient time and practice too if they are going to groove. "Sufficient" is likely to be different for different students. What is a sufficient amount of practice for Tom might be just getting started for Rachel. One day "What PCAs did you groove today?" might become another question around the dinner table.

Perhaps, for example, Maurice can control the variability of the letters "d", "o", "g" to produce the word he intends but he runs into problems when the letters look like "D", "O", "G". When Lucy is learning to swim she will need lots of opportunities of swimming in different conditions in order to become a proficient swimmer. She could swim in still water and surf, in shallow water and deep water, by herself and with lots of different people. All these different swimming experiences will help her groove her abilities so that she can move around in the water the way she wants. It's a shame that "play" seems to have acquired a frivolous, kind of non-essential connotation. "Oh, he's just playing". Perhaps, from a PCA perspective we could think of playtime as a very necessary and "groovy" activity.

Learning then is what happens when people put together PCAs so that they perceive and control things in a way that they couldn't before. Sometimes this requires a PCA that wasn't there before. When a young child learns to walk or talk or when a student learns to read they may need to create entirely new PCAs.

At other times, however, learning might simply be a change in one of the components of a PCA or a change in the connections between PCAs. When I discovered that this symbol ":-)" was a smiley face on its side it is likely that I just established a new benchmark or standard for that particular combination of symbols. I already had PCAs in place concerned with communicating in written form and I already knew what a smiley face was. The learning in this instance then, may simply have been connecting already established PCAs in ways that had not been established previously. As children progress through school this second type of learning will probably be the most common. Rather than building PCAs they didn't have before they'll be learning to put PCAs together in different ways. PCAs higher up the chain will send different standards down to other PCAs or hook up with PCAs they hadn't used before. This might explain why the learning in the younger grades is so crucial to success later on. You can't make castles in the air if you didn't gather enough bricks to start with.

When young children increasingly refine their labels of animals they are developing an ever-increasing number of animal categories. Initially they may call all animals "dog" but gradually they learn to call non-dog animals by their appropriate labels such as "cat", "pig", and "armadillo".

As Lachlan learns to paint in a cubist rather than an impressionist style he is learning to send different "As" down to lower level PCAs. He is already able to perceive different art styles, he has a reference for the kind of artwork he wants to see, and he has no trouble comparing what he is seeing with what he wants to see. What he needs to learn is to perceive himself moving the brush *this* way not *that* way. That is, he is learning to set new standards for his brush-stroking PCAs.

To learn is to construct and maintain new PCAs. It is likely that the students you teach will all differ in terms of the PCAs they have in place as they interact with the material you provide. Regardless of where they start, they will be learning to do the same thing. They will be learning to control the tasks they undertake with respect to the standards, goals, and benchmarks they have set for themselves. They will control the matching of animal pictures to animal labels, or the persuasiveness of an advertisement, or the detail in a scientific model, or the clarity and confidence in their oral presentation. Redefining learning as a process of acquiring new PCAs or reconfiguring and reconnecting existing PCAs provides us with exciting opportunities for considering curriculum delivery in schools.

It is my suggestion to you in this book that teachers will best help learning to the extent that they are able to provide students with opportunities to improve their control abilities. While students are at school they learn to control in ways that they couldn't before. To do this they need to build or mold PCAs. That is, they learn to perceive, compare, and act.

Treating students as though they are creatures who act on their environments to control perceived states of that environment is to treat students the way they are designed. When students are treated the way they are designed, more satisfying relationships are possible and greater student learning outcomes can be realized. A student's task at school is to learn to control certain perceptual variables. A teacher's task is to provide the opportunities whereby this might happen. With a clearer idea of what is actually occurring during the learning process you might be in a better position to help both your students and yourself undertake the business of learning and teaching more proficiently.

So, now that I have unpacked PCAs a little bit, for the remainder of the book I will describe how teachers might best promote student learning from this perspective. I will continue to assume throughout the book that control is all there is. Classrooms are places where a number of people are all controlling. In order to understand this environment more clearly, the notion of PCAs is all you need. The idea of a network of PCAs is what I use to inform the strategies and procedures that I describe in subsequent chapters. So, let's get on with it.

4

Tying Up a Few Loose Ends

*If you read this chapter
you'll find out why
control is important and
learn some general terms
for different aspects of control*

Tying Up a Few Loose Ends

I know I said we were about to get started on the business of applying this new way of thinking about learning but I've got to this place in the book and I have the feeling that there might be some things that need tidying up before we proceed. If you already know quite a bit about the PCA approach to control you could skip this chapter and start reading about the application of these ideas in educational settings. But if this is all new to you, then I need to clarify and explain some details before we go any further. I hope this won't be too dreary. My purpose in providing this information is to make reading and applying the rest of the book a lot easier.

The first thing to clear up is the whole issue of control. I wouldn't be surprised if, as you were reading the first three chapters, you had a little niggly voice saying something like "But why do we need to control anyway?". Unfortunately, the concept of control has had a lot of bad press over the years and it's generally considered to be something that people should try to do less of. People who are laid back and easygoing seem to be admired, and letting go of control is often suggested as a solution to people when they have problems such as relationship difficulties. I've already explained that we all control all the time, but that idea might not sit well with people who have long thought of control as an undesirable trait.

We couldn't live without control, because we exist in environments that constantly change. Our skill at controlling actually can make it hard to see what's going on, because the whole process becomes virtually invisible. We are so good at keeping things in their just-right states that, to a very large extent, we don't even notice that this is what we are doing. Think for a moment though, what would you and your immediate environment look like if the forces of nature were given free reign? If you did nothing to affect your appearance between now and next week what would you think of the image looking back at you in the mirror when you peered in at the end of seven days?

We have to control because no one else is going to do it for us! No one else knows exactly how things should be so that they are just right from our individual perspective. Even if Hamish knows Angela better than anyone else he still doesn't see things the way Angela does or feel things the same way Angela does. His hearing ability is probably different in some way, and he'll have tastes and preferences that differ to a greater or lesser extent. No one else can do this living thing for us.

So we all live in our own unique environments. Those environments frequently involve lots of other people who are also living in their own unique environments. Our environments are in a constant state of change. The saying "You never step into the same stream twice" sums it up.

Even something as commonplace as drinking a cup of coffee can be instructive when it comes to learning about control. As Kayla sips her latte, it turns out that her actions are slightly different every time she lifts the cup to her lips. This isn't just because Kayla likes to stand out from the crowd and do things differently. It's a physical necessity, because the coffee cup changes a little bit each time Kayla sips from it. With less coffee in it after each sip, the cup progressively weighs a little less. If Kayla used exactly the same actions on the last sip as she had used on the first sip, she would miss her mouth! Luckily, Kayla doesn't need to worry about figuring all this out. That's what her PCAs are for. She just decides she wants another sip of coffee and the PCAs do the rest.

PCAs are the perfect devices for being able to live in fluctuating circumstances. Bob needs to alter his actions every day he drives to work because the conditions on the road are never the same twice. The traffic is different, the weather is different, and so on. If Bob used exactly the same muscle movements to drive his car on Tuesday that he used when he drove on Monday, he wouldn't get past the end of his street before he crashed.

So this whole control show is a not an optional affair. If living things are to continue living on this planet that we inhabit then they *have to* control. Death and dying, in fact, can be thought of as the time when control stops. Living things control and non-living things don't. A rock doesn't care what you do to it because rocks don't control. If you push on a rock it moves in direct proportion to the amount of force you apply. If you push on living things, however, you never know what will happen. What will happen will depend upon the effect you've created for one or more of their PCAs.

A little bit of terminology might help here. I've already used some of the terms that are common in the PCA world but it might help to explain them and introduce some more at this stage. This will help to discuss the importance of control but it will also help for the rest of the book. None of the terms are very difficult or mysterious but introducing them will help to make sure we're on the same page when different topics are discussed.

Let's start with "perception". This word is used as a collective term to represent all those sights, sounds, sensations, feelings, and knowings that you have about the outside world. A rainbow after a storm is a perception, feeling the chill of a winter breeze is a perception, feeling your fingers on the computer keyboard is a perception, and watching the letters appear upon the screen is also a perception. That gooey feeling when your partner walks in the door is a perception and the suspicion that your boss is not happy with you is a perception too. Hearing your tummy rumble is a perception and admiring the freedom you have in your life is a perception.

Perceptions are vitally important. In fact, perceptions are all we know. Our world is just our perceptions (and that's a mighty big "just"). Even sometimes when we think we're just acting, we're really manipulating perceptions. When Crystal warms up and stretches before she takes to the blocks for her 100 m final, it looks like she's acting in certain ways. From Crystal's perspective, however, she's producing particular perceptions. When Crystal stretches her calf muscles it looks like she knows exactly how to place her legs and which way to lean. But the only thing Crystal really knows is the *feeling* that positioning herself in certain ways produces. A calf stretch is a feeling (which is a perception) to the person doing the stretch.

That makes the teachers of activities like figure skating and diving quite amazing. When Coach Shannon teaches Rory to do a double somersault with a twist they are coming from very different perspectives. All Coach Shannon can do is observe the way Rory's body moves through the air. All Rory knows, however, is how to create the feelings of spinning and tumbling. Somehow, from these different perspectives Coach Shannon helps Rory to groove his diving PCAs to the extent that he makes barely a bubble as he enters the water.

Perceptions are our current take on the world outside and are compared continuously to our internal standards. The collective term for these standards is "reference". Just like you turn to reference books when you want to find out some information, our internal references provide us with information about what is just right. We have references for how warm we like to be and how loved we like to be and how busy we like to be. Our references are our own. They can't be set by other people and they can't be given away. Sometimes we can adopt references that seem to match the references of other people but that's only ever a decision that can be made from the inside. History provides many examples of people who were prepared to die for the cause rather than take on the references of others.

The difference that is created when a perception is compared with a reference is known as "error" in the PCA world. Error in this sense is not a bad thing; it's just the technical term for a difference between a perception and a reference. If you want to drive at 55 mph and you notice the speedometer needle is hovering at 60 mph because of the error (the difference) you act so as to reduce the speed to your desired speed of 55. There would also be an error if the needle was pointing to 50 mph. If you expect your colleagues to reply when you say "Good morning", you'll feel an error when Candy doesn't return your salutation.

PCAs are created to minimize error. To reduce error, the PCA generates action. The consequence or outcome of the action is to make the perception more closely match the reference. It is through this continual process of minimizing error that we live our lives. Whenever there is error we change our actions in whatever way we need to until we're perceiving what we want (that is, until the perception matches the reference). Whenever there is no error, or minimal error, we keep doing what we're doing. It's not that we stop acting – we never stop acting (until we die), we just don't *change* our actions. Errors tell us to change what we're doing in some way.

When errors are hard to correct we sometimes build new PCAs or reconfigure the ones we've got. A fundamental type of learning is referred to as reorganization from the PCA perspective. Reorganization in this sense refers to the network of PCAs developing capabilities that it didn't have before. In many cases, the learning that occurs in school doesn't require such an extensive process. When Finn learns to calculate square roots he is probably just expanding his existing mathematical talents rather than acquiring some fundamentally new capability. Regardless of the type of learning that occurs, however, the same kinds of control processes will be involved. Throughout this book I'll just refer to "learning" without specifying whether we're discussing the fundamental process of reorganization or a less dramatic changing of references and recombining of perceptions.

Although the PCA network for each individual is hidden from view and cannot be directly observed by others in the outside world, it has an important and special relationship with that world. It is from this world that perceptions come and it is upon this world that we act in order to get and keep the just-rights (the references) that we have established. The outside world makes two important contributions to PCAs: it both helps and hinders them. The outside influences that assist PCAs in minimizing errors are collectively called the "feedback function". People use feedback functions to help them get what they want. If you want to get to work on time then your mode of transport will be part of your feedback function.

Hindrances to PCAs are known as "disturbances". A disturbance is just anything from the environment that alters what you are controlling independently of your own efforts. People in the bus queue are a disturbance to your control of a perception of being on the bus, the students passing notes in your class are a disturbance to your control of a perception of their attending to their work, and the boss running late for the meeting is a disturbance to your perception of getting on with your work when the meeting ends.

Importantly, it is the reference that determines entirely whether something is a disturbance or part of the feedback function. If you're working on getting a great tan, then scorching sunshine will be welcomed in your feedback function. If, however, your garden needs some good soaking rain to bring on the blossoms, then another day of sunshine will be a disturbance to your gardening plans.

This has crucial implications for teachers. Because we are part of our students' environments, then for them we can only ever be either a disturbance or part of their feedback function. If Mrs. Anstey wants her students to complete the entire worksheet before they leave class, but Prudence and Veronica want to discuss who they will play with at lunch time, then Mrs. Anstey will be a disturbance to the girls' conversation.

Tying Up a Few Loose Ends 45

Ironically, the girls will be a disturbance to what Mrs. Anstey is trying to achieve. If Taylor, on the other hand, wants to get really good at these sums then the task Mrs. Anstey has provided will be a big help to him. This worksheet will be part of Taylor's feedback function for his PCA related to these calculations.

When we act on our worlds to make our perceptions be just right we are acting to prevent things changing or varying from the way we want them to be. We've already established that if we leave things alone they will vary according to the whims of Nature. While we're happy to leave many things in Nature's capable clutches there are other things we care about. These things we do not want varying in arbitrary ways. We either don't want them to vary at all or we want them varying by our design and not others'. Those things "out there" in the environment that we act upon to control the variation of are called "controlled variables". Car speed can be a controlled variable, punctuality might be a controlled variable, noise level in the classroom could be a controlled variable, regularity of contact with friends may be a controlled variable, and assertiveness might be a controlled variable. Controlled variables could be thought of as the environmental representations of our just-right states. If we observe very carefully the environments of others we can get a sense of some of their just-rights by making some educated guesses about controlled variables. Disturbances are disturbances because they disturb controlled variables, and feedback functions help the variables be controlled.

The PCA situation isn't right or wrong, it's just the way we're put together. Understanding how it works and how pervasive it is will help us approach learning and achievement in classrooms from a new angle. As much as possible we should be striving to be part of our students' feedback functions rather than acting as disturbances to them. But since the impact of outside influences is always defined by inside references, we can never decide ahead of time which we are going to be. We might intend (set a reference) to be as helpful as possible to our students (becoming part of their feedback function) but if students have something else that's important to them, we might end up becoming a disturbance instead. PCAs are designed to push back against disturbances so, if at times you feel like you're engaged in a game of tug-of-war with one or more of your students, this might be telling you that you're a disturbance to them at this time.

Unfortunately, we can't insist or mandate that we will be helpful to others. We can't make other people want what we have to offer, and we can't make them appreciate us for our efforts. We will only ever be helpful to our students to the extent that they find us useful in their efforts to control some of the things that are important to them.

Effective teaching means finding ways to help students improve their abilities to control various concepts and ideas. Does the business of teaching seem even more remarkable to you now than it did a little while ago? The fact that so many teachers already find ways to be educationally useful to so many students is astounding and wonderful. It is my hope that, with the ideas in this book, you'll be able to be even more useful to more of your students more of the time. Perhaps, with a greater awareness of what is going on behind the scenes from a PCA perspective, you'll be able to be more considered and more systematic in your efforts to help students learn and achieve.

The more that students find teachers and schools to be useful in helping them achieve their purposes, the more they might engage with education. Perhaps they will discover that teachers and schools have uses that they hadn't even considered. With a PCA mindset, who knows where it will lead and what schools will become? Perhaps we can't yet even imagine all the possibilities. Well then, we'd better get on with it – there's not a moment to lose.

Tying Up a Few Loose Ends

5

Giving Schools a PCA Revamp

If you read this chapter you'll find out how to think about schools and what's goes on there from a control perspective

Giving Schools a PCA Revamp

Because this book is primarily for teachers in schools, we'll start thinking about what goes on in the classroom by considering the school environment in general. The PCA understanding of what we do has implications for schools as well as for the individual classrooms within them. Given what's been discussed in the previous chapters, we can approach the task of promoting learning and achievement in classrooms with the understanding that people act on their environments in order to make things be just right. Not all things. Just the things related to how they perceive, compare, and act – their PCAs. From this perspective, people's actions are designed to oppose disturbances to the just-right states of the things that matter to them in their environment. Any one person has a large combination of PCAs connected hierarchically and in parallel to form an intricate network. People can keep many things in their just-right states at the same time. People, for example, keep their bodies at the right temperature and in the right position, and they keep the noise entering their ears at the right level. They also try to have the right kind of contact with other people, the right job, and the right amount of money.

This is not to say that people never experience problems and that things don't sometimes occur that are not right. It is just to say that, because we are designed according to the PCA blueprint, our lives, to a very great degree, are the way we want them to be. Even people who are "stuck" in jobs or relationships they don't like are still controlling. There might be lots of things about the job they don't like but the job may provide them with the right amount of travel, or money, or prestige. Or perhaps the job just ensures that there is food on the table for the family. People may stay in relationships that are mostly unsatisfactory because for them being in the relationship is more right than being alone. Sometimes it seems to be OK to have things not quite right at one level because that helps PCAs at higher levels stay in their just-right states.

While our lives generally are pretty much the way we want them to be, some part of the network always requires our attention. Perhaps it's a bit like juggling a lot of balls. It's not uncommon to hear people talk about keeping a lot of balls in the air. Or, perhaps it's like tending a very large garden. It doesn't matter what time of year it is, there is always some part of the garden that needs your attention. A little pruning over here, a little replanting over there, a little cutting the grass somewhere else. Sometimes, you might be prepared to let one part of the garden get a bit run down because you're involved in an important project (important to you at least) somewhere else. If you get too involved in that project for too long, however, the run down and rambling section could very well start expanding to more parts of the garden or deteriorate to such an extent that you can't ignore it any longer. The best-kept gardens seem to be those that are tended constantly with time being spent where it is needed when it is needed.

So we know that people act on their environments in whatever way they need to in order to make what they perceive be just right according to their reference for the particular thing they are controlling. We also know that just-right can only ever be defined from the perspective of the individual doing the controlling. Only I can define what the right temperature of the shower is for me or what the right amount of salt is on my dinner. Only I know what the right shirt is to wear with my chartreuse trousers or where the right place is to go for my holidays or who the right person is to marry. Trying to tell someone else what is right for them is likely to create error somewhere in their PCA network. Even if you know Emma very well, you still don't know how she perceives the world nor how her perceptions are connected in the myriad of PCAs that she is. Even if Emma wants to please you and tries very hard to carry out your instructions, what you've asked her to do is likely to disturb some other part of her PCA network sooner or later. Emma's PCA of pleasing you might be in its just-right state but PCAs elsewhere might not be. There are certainly situations where we tell other people what to do and they find our advice very helpful. I think, though, that we overestimate to a very large degree how often advice-giving has that outcome. Mostly, people find a way around our advice. Sometimes, depending on our relationship, they might want us to think that the advice was very helpful, but ultimately they do their own thing anyway.

This has important implications whenever anyone tries to "help" another person. Doing something for someone else's own good or teaching someone else the "right" life to live are perilous pursuits unless we constantly check with the other person that what we are doing is indeed for their own good or the right life from their perspective. Helping can only ever be defined from the perspective of the helpee. For help to be helpful, the helpee needs to be in charge. The helper should be regarded as a resource that the helpee uses to make controlling easier.

Sometimes, to be sure, people do what other people tell them to do, but here, too, a number of things might be happening. I might wear the shirt my wife tells me to wear because I want to keep my marital relationship just right. I might holiday with friends at a less then perfect destination because I want contact with my friends to be just right. In each of these instances I am using shirt-wearing or holidaying in order to make higher-level perceptions match their references (be in their just-right states). The process of minimizing error is still preserved. So, people act to make things, lots of things, be just right from their perspective, or as close to just right as they can, and this can involve some trade-offs. This simple fact will be important to keep in mind as we approach educational environments from a PCA point of view.

What might schools be like if the process of control were recognized as the defining feature of living things? This is an audacious question to ask, but someone's got to do it! When discussing any environment it is perhaps necessary initially to acknowledge that certain constraints will apply. Some more terminology will help here: In a PCA world these constraints are known as "degrees of freedom". The more degrees of freedom an environment provides the easier it will be for individuals to control their experiences and the less often important experiences will be disturbed. A millionaire has significantly more degrees of freedom than a pauper. The more people a resource has to be shared between the fewer degrees of freedom there are for any particular individual. If Andrew has an individual tutor for his lessons he has more degrees of freedom with regard to his learning than Annabelle has, who shares her teacher with 29 other classmates.

In an environment called a Chinese restaurant there are constraints on the kinds of things I can eat. In an underwater environment there are constraints on how I can breathe and move. In a baseball environment there are constraints on the kinds of activities I can engage in. In fact, every environment has aspects that constrain the things that can be controlled within that environment. Before discussing the kinds of activities that can be undertaken in any particular environment it is first necessary, then, to be aware of any restrictions or limitations to the degrees of freedom that might be in place.

Constraints can certainly differ in how they are formed and in how they are implemented. Some constraints result from natural laws. Gravity is a constraint, for example, that I bear in mind when I walk near the edge of cliff tops, but I rarely think about other ways that it affects me, such as how it limits the ways in which I can get from the first to the second floor of a building, or the particular efforts involved in standing up and remaining standing. Other constraints exist by human design. The side of the road that I drive on or the kind of house I might build or where I can smoke a cigarette are all examples of some of the constraints that exist currently in some social environments. When constraints such as these are considered it's easy to see that many rules function as constraints in particular environments. Gravity could, perhaps, be thought of as one of the rules of nature and where you can and can't smoke could be thought of as one of the rules of public places. These kinds of rules exist because Nature put them there or because a person or a group put them there. Rules of the latter kind can be upheld through force and fighting or through negotiation and compromise, some are imposed arbitrarily and others are introduced by necessity through collaboration and discussion. Social constraints can become second nature so that, just as with a law of nature like gravity, we rarely think about them, it seems like that's just the way our world is.

It is certainly possible to discuss the appropriateness of various social constraints and rules and whether they might not be improved, but this book is not the place for it. In this book I just want to suggest the kinds of constraints and rules that might be necessary or useful (or both) in an environment focused on promoting the learning and achievement of young controllers. I'll leave the task of evaluating and refining these constraints to others. I am not arguing, therefore, that the rules and constraints that currently exist in schooling environments are necessary or beneficial, simply that they exist. Building something requires first acknowledging what there is to work with. Once schools have been established according to principles of control we might be in a better position to evaluate the usefulness of current rules and how best they might be modified.

What then, are the current rules and constraints that might need to be considered if we are to ensure that the design of schools is compatible with PCA-designed people? Perhaps this is a fundamental issue for schools. How can we design an environment that maximizes the degrees of freedom for individual students and teachers? That is, what kind of school would allow people to control their own experiences and also minimize the extent to which they disturb the controlled experiences of others?

Perhaps the first constraint in this kind of environment simply reflects the fact that we are undertaking to educate large numbers of young people at the same time. It would certainly be an enormous endeavor to provide the financial and other resources necessary to have an individual teacher for each student. We can assume then that the formal education of young people known as schooling is provided in large groups. Young people are grouped together according to various criteria such as age or ability. Typically, we could expect these groups of young people to be from between 15 to 30 people with one teacher responsible for the education of each group.

Furthermore we will assume that these groups of students come together at different times of the day and for different lengths of time. There is some flexibility, therefore in the way these groups are formed. The fact that they are formed however remains a given.

There are additional constraints in terms of what these young people are able to do when they come together in these groups. In these groups called classes only certain things can be learned. In other words, teachers have constraints about the material that they are able to teach students. Students cannot learn absolutely anything that they wish to learn in schools. There is certainly some variability available in how material is presented or the order in which it is presented. There are also, however, some restrictions on how much variation is permissible. Certain core subjects are compulsory, for example. Time limitations also exist as to how much time in a week can be devoted to particular subjects.

The learning then, that occurs in classrooms in a school environment is constrained in certain ways. Instruction is largely provided in groups of varying sizes, and the material that is taught is to a very large extent predetermined. Because people are designed to control their perceptual experiences, these constraints might present some problems to both students and teachers. It will certainly be the case that by the time the students enter any particular class they each will already have an existing network of PCAs that the learning material of the class will have to be incorporated into, and these networks of PCAs will not all be alike. It is intuitively obvious that the students who come together will have different interests, likes, and dislikes, and they will also learn at different rates and in different ways. The extent to which individuals in a class can vary is staggering. (This is another plug for the amazing job teachers do even without knowing about all this control stuff.)

In fact, even though the same educational opportunities might be provided to all the students in a group, learning remains an individual affair. Individual students can only make sense of the material in their own way and at their own pace. In this sense there really can be no such thing as "group goals". From a PCA perspective all we ever have are individuals controlling their own perceptual experiences.

This can be problematic when the expectation of the teacher assisting these students to learn is that they will master the material in the same way. Requiring students to learn material in particular ways will be a further restriction of their degrees of freedom. Some students will be interested in learning the material and some won't. Some students will engage in the learning activity just because they are interested in staying out of trouble and some won't. Some students will go along with whatever the teacher presents to them because they like the teacher and some won't. The students in any particular class at any particular time will all have their own PCAs with their own ways of making sense of the world and their own individual standards specifying their own just-rights.

From a PCA perspective, and thinking about the terminology introduced in the last chapter, you might have already realized that, for different students, the same information can either be a disturbance or part of their feedback function. The way material is understood will depend on what perceptions the students are controlling, with what just-right references, at that time. The likelihood that they will all be controlling the same things at the same time and for the same length of time is remote.

In schools where a PCA mindset was widespread, therefore, it would be recognized that, in any particular class, there will be some students who are interested in participating in the learning activities that are provided and some students who aren't. For some students these activities will be learning opportunities and for others they won't be. That is, for some students the activities provided will be part of their feedback function (they will help them control better) and for others they won't. Given the extent to which individuals control different things at the same time it should also be expected that students in a class can change what they are controlling, and their references for control, at any point in time. Students who were uninterested in the learning activities might become interested and students who were previously interested may lose interest. This is simply to describe the situation that always exists whenever a number of people with PCAs in their heads occupy the same environment for particular activities. It may well be the case during any social event. Even in a highly cohesive group such as a baseball team or an acrobatic troupe, it is likely that the people in the group are participating in the activity for different reasons. Some in the group might want to experience fame and adulation, others might be using this group as a stepping stone to bigger and better things, others might be in the group because that's where their friends are, others might be playing along to make their parents proud. So even though the members of the group seem to be working together and producing an outcome that none of them could produce individually, they might actually all be *doing* very different things from their own perspectives.

The situation in schools can be even more problematic since students have little opportunity to leave the school environment if they wish to. This is simply another constraint that exists for people involved in this type of education. It does mean however that there is a greater likelihood that what students are controlling is likely to be something other than participating in the activity that the teacher has provided.

When this happens, the activity occurring in the classroom may well be a disturbance to the student. Part of the deal when you're designed according to PCA principles is that you counteract or oppose the effect of disturbances.

Hence it will also be important for a school in PCA-land to recognize that, of the students who are not interested in participating in the learning activity, some students will actively oppose what is being presented. This will only apply to some students since only some students who don't participate will experience the activity as a disturbance. For other students the activity may be neither a disturbance nor part of the feedback function.

Silent reading time, for example, is an opportunity that could be provided to students to enable them to gain experiences with printed material. If Cody has a difference between the reading ability he wants to have and the current reading ability he perceives he has, silent reading time may well become part of his feedback function to help improve his ability to make sense of written information. If Lucy, however, wants to find out what her friend did on the weekend, she will experience silent reading time as a disturbance. Marcus, however, may well look forward to silent reading time because he can use this quiet time to imagine what his next piece of artwork will look like. To Marcus then, silent reading time has little to do with his reading ability – although it could be part of his feedback function for being the artist he wants to be!

So in a classroom, at any particular point in time, there will be students who are interested in participating in the learning activity and students who are not. Of those who are not interested in participating in the learning activity, there will be some students whose control of other variables disrupts the activity for other students (such as Lucy talking to her friend) and some whose control actions do not (Marcus visualizing his artwork for example). Again, I am not making a statement about whether this state of affairs is good or bad,

I am simply suggesting that this is the situation that will exist if we attempt to provide educational opportunities en masse to people with heads full of PCAs.

Given that schools have finite physical, personal, time, and financial resources, the ideal situation may be to provide an alternative place for students to be who are disrupting the learning activity. In order to maximize the possibility that the students who are interested in participating in the learning activity will get the best instruction possible, it is necessary to enable the teachers to devote their time to this task. Spending time convincing apparently recalcitrant students that it is in their best interests to participate in the current learning activity will probably be counterproductive. Teachers can certainly do much to help students find meaning in the learning activity. Allocating time, however, to convincing, coaxing, or otherwise persuading students to participate in what is being provided is likely to be a thankless task and a waste of an already limited resource.

The resource in this instance is the teacher's time. Teachers are busy enough just assisting those students who are undertaking the activity provided. To deny these students the assistance they require because attention is being diverted to nonparticipating students seems unreasonable. Education can only ever be a cooperative venture. Toddlers don't learn to walk or talk before they are ready and until they are interested. It would be fruitless to try and convince infants to walk before they were ready or capable.

Students in any one class on any particular day will be in different states of readiness because of the PCAs that come through the door with them. An important part of a teacher's job is to consider these differences when activities are planned and provided. Beyond that, however, PCA teachers would consider that their main job was to cooperate with students who are attempting to master the material provided.

What to do with students who are not presently interested in the learning opportunities the teacher is currently providing and are interfering with the learning of others is a perennial problem. Perhaps it is an inevitable feature of the educational environments called schools that we have created. It seems safe to suppose that in any large social group there will be times when, as people act to control their experiences, they will disturb the controlled experiences of one or more others. If it is accepted that it may well be impossible to prevent this situation from occurring given that we are organized along PCA lines, the issue then becomes: Are there things we can do to minimize the extent to which people disturb others, and how should we deal with disturbances when they occur? When students are disturbing others what experience do we want them to have?

There have been many solutions to this problem. Some solutions involve removing the disturbing students to another room or another school. Perhaps there are other solutions. Is it possible that students could be part of the solution generating process? Maybe there does not need to be a "one solution fits all" approach to the problem. Different situations might require different solutions. A useful starting point in arriving at an effective solution might be to understand the situation clearly. When Susan is disturbing others she is still controlling *something* even though it is not currently what Mr. Brimblecombe would like her to be controlling. I mentioned controlled variables in the last chapter. When things aren't going according to plan and you can't understand what someone else is doing, thinking about the situation in terms of controlled variables might help. The theory behind PCAs (PCT) has an activity called "The test for the controlled variable". I have provided a form called "Hunting for Controlled Variables" on page 64 that might help you think about controlled variables systematically. This approach to understanding what someone is doing can take a while to get used to but it's well worth the effort. Perhaps some other teachers in your faculty would be interested in meeting regularly to discuss this approach and practice getting better at it. Hunting for controlled variables can illuminate situations that previously seemed unfathomable. Once an individual's controlled variables are more accurately understood, what to do next might be more apparent also.

So, in many ways, PCA schools will look like other schools. They will have many of the same constraints that other schools have. They will be places where students will be required to attend for predetermined periods of time. They will be places where educators will be required, for the most part, to provide learning activities to groups of students rather than to individuals. Teachers in PCA schools will be constrained in the type of activities that are provided. They will only be able to provide learning activities of certain types and about certain things.

Having accepted that these are the boundaries within which education will occur it is important to keep in mind the controlling nature of individuals within these environments. At a school level, it might be ideal to provide an alternative place for students to be when they are impeding the undertaking of learning activities by other students. If this is not possible at a school level, individual teachers may still be able to provide a place in class for students to be when they are not interested in the learning activity on offer.

A PCA teacher's job is to help willing students master the learning material provided. It is not their job to convince or otherwise persuade unwilling students to be doing something the students have no wish to do. PCA teachers don't need to create stories that the material they are presenting is essential for the students to learn or is in their best interests to learn. Instead they appreciate that no one ever knows what is in someone else's best interests unless that other individual tells them. It is certainly the case that professional educators have knowledge about what is useful information for most people to have most of the time. This knowledge, however, does not include knowledge about what will be important for individuals on a moment-to-moment basis.

Within the constraints of the PCA school environment then, students can control their own experiences. This is what students are designed to do. It is what they must do. It is what they will do. Attempts by teachers to interfere with what the student's own internal network of PCAs is controlling will be seen as counterproductive. In fact, when teachers do this they will be acting as a disturbance to the students and, because PCAs are designed to oppose disturbances, we should expect the students to push back, creating opportunities for resistance and conflict. A PCA teacher's responsibility is to be as educationally useful as they can be by creating opportunities for learning through the activities they provide.

So that's what a PCA school would be like. In the next two chapters we'll have a look at individual classrooms and what teachers can do there to promote learning and achievement. Throughout this book I'm using the terms "schooling", "educating", and "learning" in a muddled up kind of a way. For the purpose of this book in terms of explaining a PCA approach to learning and achievement in schools, the distinction is not so crucial. There are differences, however, between learning, educating, and schooling and sometimes, when problems occur, it can help to decide what the problem is actually a problem of. Being late to class and passing notes to your friend are likely to be schooling problems, might sometimes be educating problems, but are not necessarily learning problems. These different terms also point to different responsibilities. Learning is the responsibility of the learner, educating is the responsibility of the educator, and schooling is the responsibility of communities and societies. These differences and their implications for addressing the challenges faced by schools could be useful topics for faculty to discuss on a regular basis.

Hunting for Controlled Variables

What's going on?	Student's actions	Your best guess about the student's just-right	Checking it out	What happens?
Wanda talks to friends during class work time	Whispering, giggling, passing notes	Contact with friends, maintaining friendships	Change the seating arrangements of either Wanda or Ruth, sit Wanda with other students, sit her alone, ask her to do a job that involves leaving the class, give Ruth a job that involves leaving the class	She complains when I suggest she moves, she calls out to Ruth from the other side of the room. When I ask her to do a job she suggests that Ruth should go with her
Ralph is extremely slow at completing work and gets upset when it's time to change tasks	Works constantly but rarely completes all the work that is set	Being perfect, getting everything right	Set easy work that Ralph can already do, set Ralph fewer tasks, ask him to nominate how much time he'll need, tell students you want to see their worst work in this activity	When the work is easy Ralph works quicker, he finishes on time if he has less to do, he sets himself long periods of time when able to, he seemed to have fun in the "worst work" activity – thought it was odd at first but then seemed to relax and was even a bit "silly"
Sky disrupts during some activities but works well at other times	Irregularly does good work but at other times she leaves her desk or talks to other students	Task difficulty – it might be that Sky likes activities that are not too easy but not too hard either	Let Sky pick the activity she wants, set her an easy activity, set her a hard one, set one activity but then change it while she's doing it to alter the difficulty	Sky works well when she selects her own activity but she's disruptive with either easy or hard activities, she complains when I change the difficulty level during the activity but is better if I tell her to just do what she can

Note: For blank copies of this and other forms, see page 145 in this book.

Giving Schools a PCA Revamp

What's going on?

In this section write down the problem or situation you want to understand better. Don't worry about being too technical at this stage – just call it as you see it.

Student's actions

What are the actions you observe? If you can be specific here about situations, duration, and frequency that will give you some clues about how to check it out.

Your best guess about the student's just-right

Now you have to think about what things might be like from the student's perspective. What might Anderson's actions be achieving for him? What part of Shelley's environment is she controlling with her actions? How are Toby's actions making things just right for him?

Checking it out

This is where you can have some fun!! You want to find ways of gently pushing on (or disturbing) what you think the student is controlling. Think about how things would be for Sarah if what was important to her was just right. Now, what could you do to make things a little bit not right? If we were working with Goldilocks you could make her porridge a bit cold or a bit hot. That's the general idea.

What happens

Once you've done the pushing, what happens? Does the student push back? If it were Goldilocks, does she try and negate your effects on her porridge. Does she change the temperature back to the way it was before? Does she pour milk on it to cool it down or pop it into the microwave to heat it up?

Actually, any time you sense that students are opposing your efforts you can suppose that you might have inadvertently just disturbed one of their just-rights. You may have just stumbled upon a controlled variable. With a little more careful observation and checking out you can become more confident about your guess.

Of course, if the student doesn't push back, that gives you information too. If you changed the temperature of Goldilocks's porridge and she happily devoured it anyway, then you could probably rule out temperature as a controlled variable (or maybe you didn't vary the temperature enough) and start hunting for something else. So whether you're right the first time around or not, with this approach you'll still get useful information about what to do next.

Another hugely convenient thing about this way of understanding your students is that it does not rely on their verbal ability for it to be effective. Even with very young students or students with disabilities you can use the idea of gently disturbing the world you think they're creating with their actions and then observe what happens. Do they push back or do you need to guess again?

So what?

The point of this exercise is not to make you into a better manipulator of students' behavior although I suppose this technology could be used that way if you wanted to. The real value in this activity is being better able to understand your students when problems occur. From a vantage point of greater understanding you'll be in a better place to know what to do next. Now that you know friendships are important to Wanda, maybe you could arrange more group-based activities where she can work with her friends. If getting things right is important to Ralph could the focus shift from quantity to quality? Would it be OK if he worked through four problems perfectly or rushed himself and completed all ten problems without much attention to detail. If task difficulty is important to Sky can she spend more time working at the level she prefers? Is it more important for her to be engaged in some activity than to be prodded and coaxed to complete work that she finds frustrating or boring?

Many of these questions will be personal ones for teachers to reconcile with their own professional just-rights about being educationally useful. Regardless of the answers you come up with, by becoming proficient at hunting for controlled variables you can be sure that your decision-making is based on a sound and systematic procedure that is compatible with our own internal PCA organization.

6

Setting the Scene in the Classroom

If you read this chapter you'll discover how to structure the classroom environment to enable all its inhabitants to control more effectively

Setting the Scene in the Classroom

So, now we know that people in an environment, any environment, act on that environment in order to perceive it in the just-right (reference) states specified by their PCAs. Classrooms are among those environments. People in a classroom then, can generally be expected to be maintaining their perceptions in their reference (just-right) states. Teachers are included in this "people in the classroom" category. The activity of teaching involves controlling certain perceptions. What might some of these perceptions be?

In the previous chapter I introduced the idea that learning needs to be a cooperative venture. It may be the case that learning from someone else can *only ever* be a cooperative venture. Forcing someone to do what they don't want to do invites resistance and conflict. Furthermore it erodes the time that is spent assisting those students who are willing participants. In a classroom then, teachers should be spending the great majority of their time with students who are interested in learning what they have to teach.

Well then, let's get a handle on this teaching business from the PCA platform. As we've seen, to learn is to improve one's control abilities. To do this new PCAs are constructed or existing ones are reconfigured in some way. If we assume that to be the case then, teaching could be considered to be the activity that occurs when one individual attempts to help another individual improve their ability to control. The individual who is helping by teaching is part of the environment of the individual who is learning. This means that if a teacher is anything at all to a student, they are either a disturbance or part of the feedback function for particular PCAs. Teachers who want to work in a PCA world would strive to be part of the feedback functions of their students. The first thing teachers should control for then in a PCA school is to make themselves available for students to include them in their feedback functions. This is the essence of being educationally useful. To this end, teachers should minimize the extent to which they act as disturbances to students.

While it may be difficult to know precisely when you are acting as a disturbance to another person there can be general clues to indicate that this might be the case. As a teacher, whenever you sense resistance from a student, that is a good sign that you are disturbing something they are maintaining in a particular way. When this occurs you should reduce your current demands or come at it from a different angle. This is akin to dropping the rope in the tug-of-war game. For the student to learn, what is most important is the process taking place inside the student. Asking the student about what is happening is often a good way to check on the process that is occurring.

In order to increase the likelihood that as a teacher you will become part of the feedback function of the student, negotiation and compromise are two essential tools. Negotiation and compromise may well be essential tools whenever PCA people get together. If that is so in general, then it will certainly apply in the classroom. In the previous chapter we discussed some of the constraints that are characteristic of school environments and of the classrooms within those environments. These constraints could be thought of as the nonnegotiable aspects of schooling. Within the boundaries defined by these constraints, however, there is much that can be negotiated.

The concepts of negotiation and compromise are certainly not new. What may be new, however, is the understanding that a PCA awareness brings to these two methods. PCA-style negotiation and compromise are not used to induce other people to behave the way we want them to. Negotiation and compromise are simply used because these are the best ways of enabling all people in a social group to control their own experiences within the constraints of the environment. Some time back, the idea of providing choices to students became quite trendy. There was probably some merit in the original idea, but rather than being a step towards legitimate collaboration, it quickly became apparent that giving choices was being used by some teachers as a tricky way of shaping students' behavior. Teachers got into the habit of giving one nifty choice and one that wasn't so enticing. Coincidentally, the nifty choice usually involved the students behaving in the way that the teacher wanted them to. Sometimes, neither option was so great (you can finish your work now or come back at lunch time) but one was always less attractive than the other. This way of approaching choices was from the school of thought that treats people like rocks (if you push on them they'll move along according to how much force you apply). But people aren't like rocks so, not surprisingly, it wasn't long before the students wised-up to what was going on, and in the long run the approach only achieved at best luke-warm success.

The complexity of the negotiation and what gets negotiated will be influenced by the age of the students and the particular school environment you work in. In primary schools, for example, teachers could negotiate with students about when they undertake certain subject areas. Perhaps specialist lessons such as music and PE are nonnegotiable. The start and finish of the school day is likely to be nonnegotiable. As are the break times. With the nonnegotiable times clarified then, it becomes possible to identify what is negotiable. The complexity of the negotiating could vary as students become more skilled at it.

With young children a simple negotiation may be appropriate. Perhaps with young children it would be appropriate to discuss things on a day-to-day basis or even a session-by-session basis.

> Before lunch we need to do sums, spelling, and writing.
>
> Which one would be best to do first?
>
> Which one should we do last?

Perhaps discussions like this could even involve voting and discussions about what can be done when not everyone in a group thinks the same way or agrees about the same thing. These kinds of activities take a little time but they provide valuable learning experiences for students.

As a preschool teacher I conducted a music session and a language session each day with my preschool class. These sessions were at the same time everyday. I was aware, however, that at the time that I called the music or the language session any of the students may be engaged in activities that were important and beneficial to them. I decided, therefore, not to make attendance at these sessions compulsory. Students were able to decide when I announced that the session was starting whether or not they would attend. The only stipulation I had was that once the session started, if they had decided not to attend, they couldn't change their minds and begin participating in the session. Any student who didn't attend was well supervised by the teacher aide I worked with.

I implemented this system in the final year of my teaching in preschool classes. Throughout the year there were never more than two or three students who didn't attend any particular session. Furthermore, no student missed more than two or three consecutive music or language sessions. It could even be argued that had students stayed away from these sessions in large numbers or particular students stayed away for long periods of time, that would have provided me with valuable information. I could have used that information to investigate whether students were experiencing problems with language or music that I could address. I could have begun to wonder about what seemed more important to the students, and I could have started hunting for controlled variables.

With older students perhaps the whole week could be planned at the outset.

> This week we need to spend eight hours on language activities, seven hours on math activities, three hours on science activities, two hours on art activities and two hours on social studies activities. We have music at 10.30 am on Wednesday morning and PE at 2.00 pm on Thursday afternoon. How will we divide up the week?
>
> How much time each day do you want to spend on language activities?
>
> Should we do math before language or should language be first?
>
> Which subjects would be best to do in the morning when you are fresh?
>
> Which subjects could we do in the afternoon when you might be tired?

These kinds of discussions will provide students with experiences of negotiating. Teachers should ensure, however, that the discussion is a legitimate negotiation. Teachers should guard against situations where they engage students in pseudo-negotiations that are really just protracted attempts by the teacher to get their own way. The teacher needs to accept that students might have different ideas about how the week should be divided up. As long as the necessary time requirements are being observed teachers should be prepared to negotiate equally with students about when various activities will be undertaken. If there is something that you as the teacher are not prepared to budge on then don't introduce this as a topic for negotiation with your students.

This illustrates perhaps a more general principle about learning. As I've suggested, learning involves the establishment of new PCAs or new connections between existing PCAs. These PCAs arise and get connected through experience, and any seasoned teacher would recognize that students need repeated experiences in order to master learning in a particular area. We've already discussed the importance of grooving. As we provide experiences to students, it is important, therefore, to reflect on how those experiences are *experienced by students*, not as we think they should be experienced. When a teacher gives students lots of instructions and expects regular and routine obedience to these instructions, what is being experienced by the students? Could it be the case that, in this situation, students are experiencing compliance even though the teacher might be experiencing cooperation? If we want students to experience and value such things as cooperation we need to act cooperatively towards them. That is, we need to provide students with experiences of cooperation. It might even be useful to casually label the interaction as cooperation when it is happening, to draw the student's attention to the positive aspects of it. "I'm really glad you let me know how I could help you with this Sam. It makes the job easier when we cooperate together doesn't it?"

The same idea applies for negotiation and compromise. If it is important for you to always make the decisions in your class and to have outcomes the way you want them, then it will be very difficult for students to experience negotiation and compromise with you. Perhaps what they will experience would be more correctly labeled as persuasion.

At this point I'm not making a judgment about which experience is better in your class with your students. Only you can decide that based on the way you want to think about yourself as a teacher and the things you want your students to learn – that is, the just-rights that you already control and the just-rights that you'd like your students to become skilled at controlling. But when you hear teachers commenting that their students aren't cooperative or respectful enough, it is interesting to wonder about the experiences that these teachers are providing to their students. Are their classroom interactions flavored with cooperation and respect? Thinking along these lines provides useful avenues for reflection and professional development. – Are the experiences you provide your students consistent with the learnings you'd like them to have?

When negotiations are conducted, teachers should not facilitate a particular process arriving at a specific outcome. The more a teacher has a certain result in mind the greater is the likelihood that they will act to realize it. Instead, the purpose of the negotiation is to find a way of satisfying all parties. Certainly no result will ever be perfect for everyone in the class all the time. That is the reason that compromise is necessary. Again, these kinds of negotiated discussions give teachers a good opportunity to provide students with experiences of compromise.

> Are we all going to be able to get exactly the times that we want this week?
>
> If some people want to do language first and some people want to do math first how will we come to a compromise?
>
> Well, I'd really prefer to do language in the morning but if most of the class want to do it after lunch, I'd be willing to compromise. I'd be prepared to do language after lunch as long as we can do it before math. Would that be OK?

Sometimes teachers might want to avoid situations where students are in competition. However, whether it is beneficial or detrimental, competition is a part of some types of human interactions. Again, as a preschool teacher, it seemed to me to be a better idea to teach students how to deal with competition rather than to avoid it. We therefore, had two classroom tasks to be completed each day by individual students. One task was helping me mark the class roll and the other task was to collect the lunches. Students enjoyed the opportunity to do either of these tasks. Each day then the students would nominate some students to be assigned the tasks. We would then vote for the two students who would carry out the tasks for that day. At the end of every voting session I would always ask students some questions that helped them reflect on the voting process.

> If you didn't get voted for the jobs today does that mean you'll never get voted to do the jobs?
>
> What can you do tomorrow if you want to have a turn at doing the jobs?
>
> Does it mean that you're not a nice person if you didn't get voted to do the jobs?

The assigning of tasks and the voting process were simply experiences that provided us with opportunities to discuss some aspects of social living.

These sorts of experiences will give students the opportunity to learn about the give and take that is such a necessary part of satisfying social relationships. By negotiating and compromising, teachers are ensuring that they have done all that they can to assist students to control their own experiences within the constraints of the educational environment. They will only have done this, however, if the negotiation and compromise are legitimate activities.

There's no doubt that negotiation and compromise could be used as subtle attempts for teachers to introduce predetermined procedures. It might be useful to think about how the students experience this. If the outcome is already determined, then a negotiation and compromise cannot legitimately be entered into. It is perhaps best in these situations to be up-front with students and explain the reason behind the necessary introduction of the procedure. Thinking about people as controllers will help teachers better understand the interactions that can occur in their class. Cooperation from a PCA perspective, for example, could be thought of as an interaction where two (or more) people are each part of the feedback function of the other. That is, I'm helping you make things just right for you, and you're helping me do the same. When one person follows another's instructions, however, and the person giving the instructions has no regard for the just-rights of the other, this interaction is characterized by compliance rather than cooperation.

When negotiation and compromise are undertaken all individuals involved should generally be able to get some of what they want. Where the process is used, however, for teachers to introduce the plans they had already conceived, it is difficult to think of two-way negotiation and compromise occurring. Thinking in PCA terms might help you evaluate what interactions you are promoting in your classroom and how these interactions might be experienced by your students.

To what extent are students able to determine their own experiences, within the constraints of the environment at the moment?

How will I react if students suggest something that I'm not entirely happy with, but that is still within the guidelines?

Am I engaging in this activity because I want students to do what I want?

A recording sheet has been provided at the end of this chapter to help you to introduce negotiation and compromise into your class.

Negotiation and compromise is perhaps even more relevant with adolescents than it is with younger children. Schools for teenagers should be based on the same principles that we've already discussed. Some things are negotiable and others are not. Students, for example, could choose subjects within a certain range of choices. The times during the week that these subjects are offered, however, might not be negotiable.

Even within the one subject there are opportunities to negotiate some aspects of the curriculum. Perhaps over a semester four units of work need to be covered. The units might take five weeks each. Again, class groups could negotiate the order in which they completed their units. Perhaps in English there may be a choice of two or three novels that students could read for assessment. Do all students have to read the same novel at the same time or is there scope for flexibility here?

Perhaps the nature of assessment tasks could be negotiated. If students are required to give oral presentations could there be some wiggle room about the nature of the presentation – could it be given individually as a short talk or in a group as a debate? Could students make some decisions about the weighting of their assessment? Could students who are better at written work than exams elect to weight their assignments more heavily, and those who like exams put a greater weighting there?

For the unit you're starting next week, could you even ask students how they'd prefer that you introduced it?

> Next week we're starting a unit about town planning and we'll be looking at how to create livable cities for large numbers of people with sustainable communication and transport networks. How should we get started with this? What are the first things you'd like to know about this unit?

Negotiation and compromise should not be seen as a one-time activity but, rather, should become the general method of communication within a classroom. Negotiating classroom rules and procedures at the beginning of the year and then resuming a position of authority and directiveness is not likely to bring about much change. There are many potential opportunities throughout the day, week, and year for negotiation and compromise. Who decides, for example, where students sit in your class?

The extent to which negotiation and compromise pervade school classrooms is limited only by the ingenuity of the teachers who reside there. I have already demonstrated how very small children can be involved in these activities. Even non-verbal students and students with disabilities can be immersed in negotiation and compromise. With their knowledge of the functioning of PCAs, teachers who know about control could be sensitive to the times they act as a disturbance to their students. Even students who can't talk will let you know when you are disturbing them. Sometimes, the messages you get from them about your disturbing effects are clearer and louder than the messages from their more verbal counterparts. The bottom line, I guess, is that if you think this control stuff is important, you'll find a way to acknowledge it and honor it in your classroom. It's the "All roads lead to Rome" idea (the same idea is expressed in the not very politically correct saying "There's more than one way to skin a cat"). In not too long *you* might be telling *me* about the innovative ways you've invited control into your classroom. I would love nothing more than for the ideas in this book to become old-fashioned as teachers find creative ways of curriculumizing control.

The role of PCA teachers is to make themselves available as learning resources for students. To be educationally useful, it is their role to help students make sense of particular learning material. In this way, teachers are helping students learn to control their experiences more effectively. Again, this can only ever be a cooperative venture.

At a general level then teachers need to give students as much information as they can about the types of experiences they will be encountering at school. The more information a person has, the more easily they are able to fit new experiences into their existing network. Imagine how difficult it would be to drive along a winding unfamiliar road at night in a thick fog.

The same road would be much easier to drive along on a clear day. Teachers can do much to take the guesswork out of the school day for students. Students will be able to control more effectively if they know what's coming up around the next corner.

Even once the session, daily, weekly, or semester timetable has been negotiated, teachers can still do things to assist students. On a lesson-to-lesson basis simply giving students information at the beginning of the lesson to let them know what will be happening will allow them to predict what is coming. Explaining things like what the lesson will be about, how long it will take, how it relates to other lessons, and the tasks that will be provided for students to complete helps students know what is ahead and enables them to prepare. Keeping this information from students is asking them to drive in a fog.

Thinking of your students as critters who are designed to control will help you structure the classroom environment so that you maximize the extent to which you are part of their feedback functions and minimize the extent to which you are a disturbance to them. In a climate such as this you are likely to be educationally useful to more of your students more of the time. Thinking of yourself and your students as controllers and getting comfortable with the PCA world that we can't step out of will help you understand classroom relationships and interactions differently. From this understanding will emerge experiences that are just right for both teachers and learners in schools.

Chapter Six

Increasing Experiences of Negotiation

Date: _____

PRENEGOTIATION

How much negotiation occurs between my students and me? (circle one)

    a little   some   a lot

1   2   3   4   **(5)**   6   7   8   9   10

How much negotiation would my students say occurs in our class?

    a little   some   a lot

1   2   **(3)**   4   5   6   7   8   9   10

How much negotiation would I like to occur between my students and me?

    a little   some   a lot

1   2   3   4   5   6   7   **(8)**   9   10

What aspects of the school and classroom program are nonnegotiable?
1. When we start and finish
2. The time for morning tea and lunch
3. The importance of safety
4. School uniforms
5.

What aspects of the school and classroom program can be negotiated?
1. When we do subjects
2. How much homework I give out
3. Arrangement of desks and where students sit
4. Amount of groupwork v individual work and who does what
5.

What will I negotiate first?
    Arrangement of desks and seating

Do I have an outcome I would prefer?   **(YES)**   NO

If yes, what is my preference?
    I'd prefer the desks to be in rows

Note: For blank copies of this and other forms, see page 145 in this book.

Setting the Scene in the Classroom

What will I do if students suggest things I'm not entirely happy with?
Listen to their reasons, explore consequences, focus on important goals (and try hard not to persuade them to my way of thinking)

When will I conduct the negotiation?
In the morning after we come in

How long do I expect the negotiation to take?
20 minutes

What sorts of questions will I ask during the negotiation?
Why do we need desks? What do we come into class for?
Are you happy with the current seating arrangement?
How can we arrange the desks to make learning better?

POSTNEGOTIATION

My overall impression was that the negotiation session was:

unsuccessful   somewhat successful   **(very successful)**

Generally, I was happy with the way I:
I maintained a 'curious', 'inquisitive', even 'playful' attitude during the negotiation and I think that played a big part in why it was as enjoyable as it was.

To improve future negotiations I could:
Keep them shorter, ask specific questions to specific students rather than general questions to the whole class, ask more students questions.

The next thing I will negotiate is:
Amount of homework

I will conduct this negotiation on:
Friday week

7

Going About the Business of Teaching

If you read this chapter you'll learn about your role as a PCA teacher and the kinds of tasks this involves

Going About the Business of Teaching

So far we've discussed the way the general school environment could be structured and I've suggested that schools are environments that are characterized, at least in part, by certain constraints or limitations to the degrees of freedom for individuals. (That includes all individuals – teachers and students and administrators too!) We've also discussed what a classroom environment might be like in PCA-land. Again, certain constraints will be in place. Within those constraints, however, it's likely that negotiation and compromise could be used much more than they currently are. Negotiation and compromise are perhaps the methods of choice when trying to figure out how PCA creatures might get along together in a specific social group with specific tasks.

In this chapter we'll narrow the focus yet again to consider how a teacher might undertake the business of teaching from a PCA perspective. Perhaps, in the last chapter, some of the strategies we discussed were already familiar to you. What may have been novel, however, was the PCA understanding behind these strategies. A bit like changing from watching ships sail out to sea with a flat earth understanding, to watching them sail away with the knowledge that the world is a globe. The same thing might happen in this chapter. Some of what we discuss you might already be familiar with at a procedural level. What might be novel, however is the PCA understanding behind these approaches.

To discuss sensibly how teachers should go about doing their job in a PCA school we should first lay our cards on the table about what a PCA teacher's role is. Tom Bourbon is a good friend of mine and one of the giants of Perceptual Control Theory (PCT – you remember, that's the theory behind all this control stuff). Quite provocatively (perhaps), Tom summed up a teacher's role like this: "No one is responsible for anything that anyone else does. Teachers cannot 'teach' students (in the sense of making them change in a certain way) to 'follow the rules', or to 'be responsible citizens', or to 'control without disturbing others', or to do, or be, anything at all. All teachers can do is control to perceive themselves doing things…" From this simple quote you may get an even better sense of how different the idea of PCA education is. Different, and profoundly challenging perhaps.

The role of a PCA teacher, then, would be defined by the perceptions that people in this role might control. PCA teachers should have certain just-rights. From a PCA perspective, teachers cannot "produce" behavior in students in terms of producing good academic grades or good class control. All that will be assumed to happen in a classroom is that teachers and students are controlling their own perceptions. Teachers in PCA schools, therefore, would not be held accountable for either the academic or social behavior of students. You can't be held accountable for something you can't control. That would be like holding people accountable for the weather. That's not to say, however, that teachers should be absolved of all responsibility. Teachers would be held accountable for the perceptual experiences they create and maintain in class. If that sounds a bit highfalutin to you, read on – the practical translation is provided below.

We know now that all someone can ever be to another person is a disturbance, part of their feedback function, or nothing at all with respect to what the person is controlling. Understanding the task of PCA teaching does not diminish the importance of the teacher's role. It simply allows for a more accurate portrayal of what is happening.

As PCAs themselves, teachers create and maintain certain perceptual experiences in the classroom. That's not good or bad or right or wrong – it just is. Teachers can't help but control their experiences, that's what they're designed to do. Well, they can't help it as long as they're alive, and a dead teacher isn't much good to anyone.

So, the big deal about all this is that teachers have to control *some* perceptions while they are in the class (just as they control perceptions in their life outside the class).

What should these perceptions be?

Teachers could, for example, decide to adopt references (just-rights) about the grades students should get, or the way they should behave in class.

What might some of the consequences of controlling these perceptions be?

If teachers wish to see students in their classes achieve good academic grades, then certain responses from students on exams and other pieces of assessment will be their just-rights. Mrs. Norvil might have a reference, for example, to see 70% of her class achieve a grade of "B" or higher. In this instance, she will perceive, compare, and act with respect to student grades. She will perceive the grades the students are achieving and compare this with the grades she wants the students to achieve. She will then act on her environment in order to make what she perceives match what she wants to perceive. For this example she will need to act on the students in order to somehow "elicit" high grades from them. In other words, Mrs. Norvil will need the students to act in particular ways in order for them to create the perception she has specified. In this situation, therefore, Mrs. Norvil will need to evaluate the behavior of her students in order for her to maintain her perceptions in their reference (just-right) states. There's nothing mysterious about this. We all know this by now. This is all hum-drum, bread and butter, good old-fashioned PCAs doing their control thing.

The only glitch in an otherwise perfect plan is that the students whose behavior Mrs. Norvil is evaluating are all PCAs too. Could it be the case that at some point, some students may have different ideas about their behavior than the ideas Mrs. Norvil has?

If teachers are attempting to see students act in ways that are at odds with what the students intend, how might the students experience the teacher's efforts? Isn't it likely that the teacher's actions would be a disturbance to the perceptions that the students are controlling?

(That's a series of those annoying rhetorical questions where you and I both know what the answers should be. I've included them for emphasis, though, rather than annoyance!)

Now let's consider Mr. Livron. Let's say he's been to a workshop and learned all about the theory (PCT) and about control and he's quite intrigued by the idea that we're designed as PCAs. He's decided a suitable just-right might be about helping students achieve the grades that they want to achieve. With his PCA bearings set on this course, he will perceive, compare, and act with respect to helping. He will pay attention to (perceive) how much he is helping and compare this with the amount of help he thinks is just right and he will act so as to maintain his perception of helping in its reference state. In this situation then Mr. Livron will rate the extent to which he is helping rather than the behavior of his students. That is, he will evaluate himself rather than his students. Along the way, he might even learn some things about the amount of help he distributes to different students. Perhaps he discovers he needs different just-rights for different students and maybe he gets better at giving more appropriate amounts and kinds of help to his students. With a reference of helping, then, both Mr. Livron and his students will all be more likely to be able to control their own experiences within the constraints of the environment, rather than having their experiences specified for them.

Going About the Business of Teaching

We can perhaps imagine some of the dinnertime conversations in their respective homes: At Mrs. Norvil's place she might be asked

> "So how was your day honey?"

and she could reply with

> "Oh, it was great. You know, almost all my kids got As and Bs on that test I gave them."

or

> "Oh, not so good. I just don't know what I'm doing wrong. My kids bombed out on that test I gave them."

While at Mr. Livron's place he might be asked

> "So how was your day honey?"

and he could reply with

> "Oh, it was great. You know, I got around the whole class and helped them with the work they were doing."

or

> "Oh, not so good. I just couldn't seem to help a couple of the kids. I'm going to have to think some more about coming at it differently."

With an understanding of control, PCA teachers would set goals about the experiences that they would like to create and maintain in class rather than the experiences they think their students should be creating and maintaining. Teachers will be interested in constantly monitoring how educationally useful they are being to students. Teachers might have goals about a number of things. The defining feature of these goals however would be that the teachers would be evaluating themselves rather than their students. That is, the goals would not require the students to act in any particular way. Teachers might, for example, set goals about the number of questions they ask or the number of activities they provide or the extent to which they incorporate opportunities to negotiate into their classroom procedures. They might also be interested in the number of different modalities in which they present learning opportunities, or the extent to which they link new learning opportunities to previously presented material. Also, they could perhaps set goals about how much effort they put into acquiring knowledge of the backgrounds and interests of their students. They could also strive to use this knowledge in the preparation of the learning opportunities they provide. Furthermore they could set goals about the extent to which they incorporate goal-setting as part of classroom activities.

A teacher's role in a PCA school would center around being as helpful to the students as they could be. Once again, the kind of help that teachers are able to offer will be constrained by the environment they are in. Knowing this, teachers would set goals about the work they do in and out of class, rather than goals about the work their students should do. A planning sheet (PCT-Based Lesson Plan) at the end of this chapter will help teachers identify goals to create and maintain in class. Teachers who understood PCA principles would not need the students in their class to act in any particular way for them to be able to experience competence and professionalism in their role.

Competence and professionalism for teachers interested in the brave new PCA world are realized through the opportunities that they provide for students. Teachers in these schools would work hard at providing the learning opportunities that have the best chance of being interesting and meaningful for students. To do this they would structure their lessons around the ideas of learning that we've been discussing here. Lessons will be concerned with helping students control particular perceptual variables more effectively. The PCT-Based Lesson Plan at the end of this chapter may be a useful instrument to assist you in structuring your lessons this way, or it might give you some ideas with which you can create your own even more useful form.

At the end of a lesson PCA teachers would evaluate how useful the students found the opportunity they provided. That is, to what extent was the opportunity experienced as an opportunity by the students? They would then use this information as the basis for planning further learning opportunities for students. It might seem at this point that the teacher is focusing on the behavior of the students to make the evaluation. It is true that the teacher is interested in the behavior of the students as information for the planning of future lessons. The point to understand here, however, is that the teacher is not attempting to produce any *particular* behavior in the students. In fact, the teacher is not attempting to produce any behavior at all in the students. The teacher wants to help the students. That's all. As has been mentioned, the help that the teacher can give will be limited by the constraints of the environment. Within those constraints, however, teachers will work hard at being as helpful as they can be. In essence then, what they evaluate at the end of the lesson is the extent to which they have helped. Not the extent to which students have behaved in particular ways.

Of central importance is to remember that the lessons are designed to assist students to control certain variables. Spending time identifying the variables involved in the subject matter you are teaching can give you a clearer sense of just what the students will need to learn to do if they are to master the material. Learning to do long division, for example, is learning to control a sequence of steps. Learning to produce scientific reports requires being able to control variables related to structure and writing style. Spending time, therefore, identifying the important variables that underpin the subject matter you are presenting will be time well spent. The opportunities provided by teachers will essentially enable students to be active in the learning process. Obviously, if students are to become proficient at controlling particular variables they need groove time, time to repeatedly practice keeping these variables in their reference (just-right) states.

The hierarchical arrangement of PCAs will be another useful fact to keep in mind when planning lessons or units of work. For students to grow a PCA to control what you're teaching them, they'll need to be able to fit this new PCA into their existing network. While you're planning, therefore, it might help to think about the PCAs that will be above and below the PCA you want the students to insert. The use of "why" and "how" questions can be very useful in helping you think about where this new PCA might best fit. *Why* questions give you an idea of what's above the current consideration and *how* questions give you a sense of what's going on underneath.

If we applied these ideas to your reading of this book, a conversation like the following might occur

>Why are you reading this book?
>
>>To become a better teacher
>
>Why do you want to become a better teacher?
>
>>To help students learn
>
>Why do you want to help students learn?
>
>>So that they can make something of their lives
>
>Why do you want your students to make something of their lives?
>
>>Because that will make the world a better place

If you follow the why thread for very long you get to some pretty important places! A conversation going the other way might unfold like this

Going About the Business of Teaching

How are you reading this book?

> I'm just setting aside some time each night to read a couple of pages

How are you setting aside time each night?

> I've told my family that from 8.00 to 8.30 pm is my reading time and not to disturb me

How did you tell your family that?

> I waited until we were all together at dinner and then I discussed with them what I wanted

How questions can get some pretty specific answers and can also involve a number of different paths. Another conversation might have been

How are you reading this book?

> I'm reading a couple of pages at a time and making notes in the margins

How do you make the notes?

> Whenever something grabs my attention I make a little comment or put a little star beside the text

How do you decide what grabs your attention?

> If I read something that's different from what I expected and I have to think about it, I mark that out so I can come back to it later

The same kind of process could be used with your unit planning. It's important when you do this that you think about the answers from the students' perspective and not yours. So if you were asking yourself "Why would my students want to learn long division?" or "Why would my students want to learn about the Pre-Raphaelite artists?", the answer (from their perspective) probably wouldn't be "Because it's in the curriculum". Thinking about these questions might not be easy but they will help you to make sense of the curriculum material for your students.

Similarly, thinking about how questions "How will my students master constructing Haiku poetry?" or "How will my students create the perfect soufflé?" will give you a sense of the necessary skills and knowledge (bunches of PCAs) that you're assuming they'll have before you start. Spending time going down these paths might help you predict some of the difficulties that students in your class will have and how best you might help them overcome these obstacles.

With both the why and the how questions you might notice that a number of different paths could be followed. That's OK. There's no right and wrong with this, and different students may well have different answers to these questions. Spending time thinking of some of the possible answers, however, may help you plan activities and experiences that will be meaningful, engaging, and helpful to your students.

In closing this chapter, I should emphasize that there is nowhere to hide with this approach. Because we are designed to push back against disturbances, you will get a good sense of the just-rights that you have in the school environment by becoming more aware of the things that bother you. You might have convinced yourself that you are really only interested in controlling the things you can control, but have a think about the things that raise your dander during the school day. Do you tend to notice the tone of voice of your students or do you monitor your own quality of expression? In conversations with your colleagues do you tend to discuss the behavior of your students or your own efforts to be helpful? The things that tend to bother you and the things that dominate your attention will give you useful and important information about the PCAs that *actually* exist inside you, regardless of the ones you'd like to think are in there.

Once you have an appreciation of where you're currently at, if you're not enchanted with this place you'll be able to move somewhere better.

PCT-Based Lesson Plan

My goal for this lesson is to experience myself:
    Being inspirational and amazing. I want to make sure I ask every student at least one question. I want to smile a lot (in a natural way not a forced way) and I want to keep the volume of my voice low.

The standards I will be using to measure how effectively I control these perceptions are:
    I'll rate on a scale from 1 (being 'low') to 10 (being 'high') my levels of 'inspirationality' and 'amazingness' at least 3 times throughout the lesson. I want to be 8 out of 10 on both of them. I'll keep a note of all the students of whom I ask questions. I want to have a natural smile on my face 80% of the time and I want to keep my voice volume at 5 or lower (on a scale from '1 = whisper' to '10 = bellow') for the entire lesson.

In this lesson I will be providing opportunities for students to control what variable?
    Correct identification of 7 sight words

To what extent do students already perceive this variable?
    They know what a word is and they know different words have different shapes. Also they mostly all know almost all their letters and letter sounds.

Are students able to remember this variable?   NO

What evidence is there for this?
    Well they know some words already so they know what words are. They also can remember the days of the week so they can remember 7 things.

Is there a reference state of this variable?   NO
What is it?
    Correctly matching the written word with its verbal name e.g., seeing "play" written on a card and saying "play".
    For students to develop literacy, the eventual reference state is to identify all 7 words with no more than a 1 second delay between presenting the written word and saying the word.

Note: For blank copies of this and other forms, see page 145 in this book.

What opportunities will I provide students to experience this reference state?
Lots of presentations of the words. Pictures of the words. Drawing activities with drawing the words in different colours. Writing the words in the air with their fingers. Making letters out of play dough and forming the words.

Are the students able to compare the reference state to other states of this variable? (YES)   NO

What opportunities will I provide for students to make these comparisons?
Holding the words upside down. Showing them similar words (e.g., 'is', 'it', and 'in')

Are the students able to make the necessary adjustments to ensure what they perceive is kept in its reference state? YES   (NO)

What opportunities will I provide for students to make these adjustments?
Use magnet letters to let them make words right (e.g., put up the letters "anf" or "an" and ask them to make other words such as "and" and "ant")

How much grooving have students been able to do to practice keeping this variable in its reference state?

a little   (some)   a lot

What grooving opportunities will I provide for students to practice keeping this variable in its reference state under different conditions?
Make packs of cards for students to take home to practice with their parents. Have our teacher assistant take students in groups of 2 or 3 to practice. Put words up around the classroom.

What information did I obtain from this learning opportunity that I will use to help me plan subsequent opportunities?
Different levels of students – some students can go on to more words, other students need more time making up words with play dough, magnetic letters, etc.

102 Chapter Seven

Fitting PCAs Into the Network – Whys

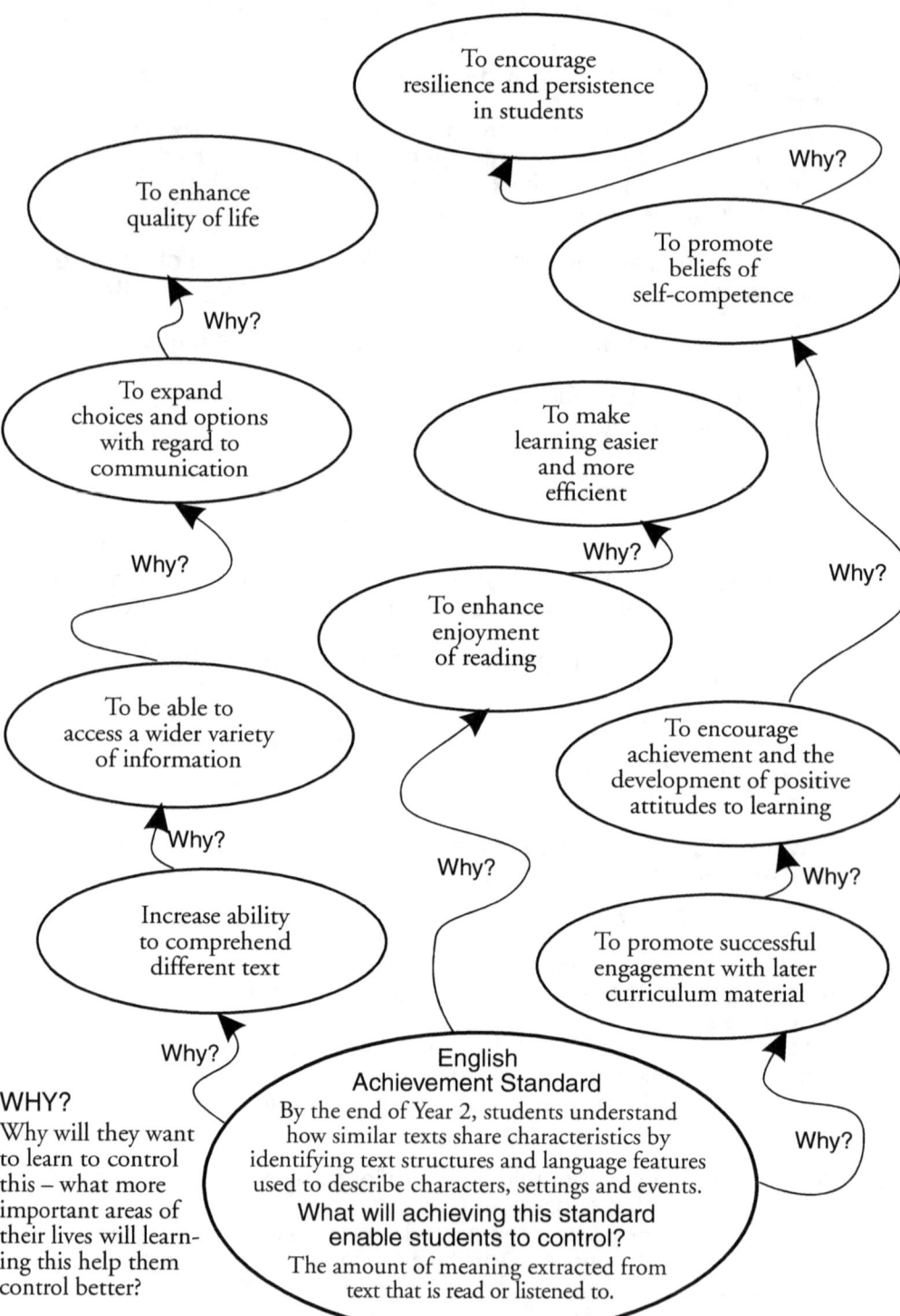

Note: For blank copies of this and other forms, see page 145 in this book.

Going About the Business of Teaching

Fitting PCAs Into the Network – Hows

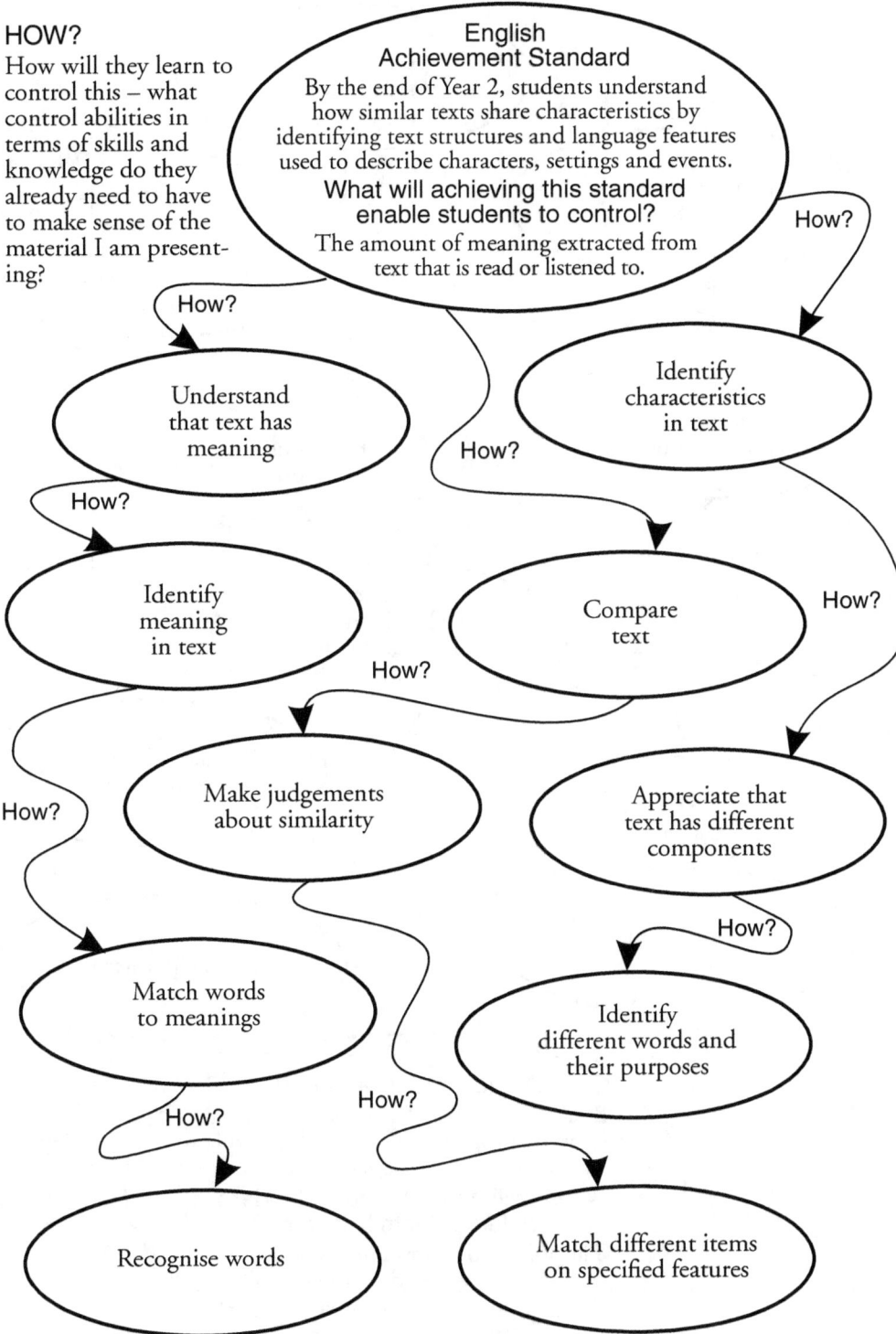

104 Chapter Seven

Fitting PCAs Into the Network – Whys

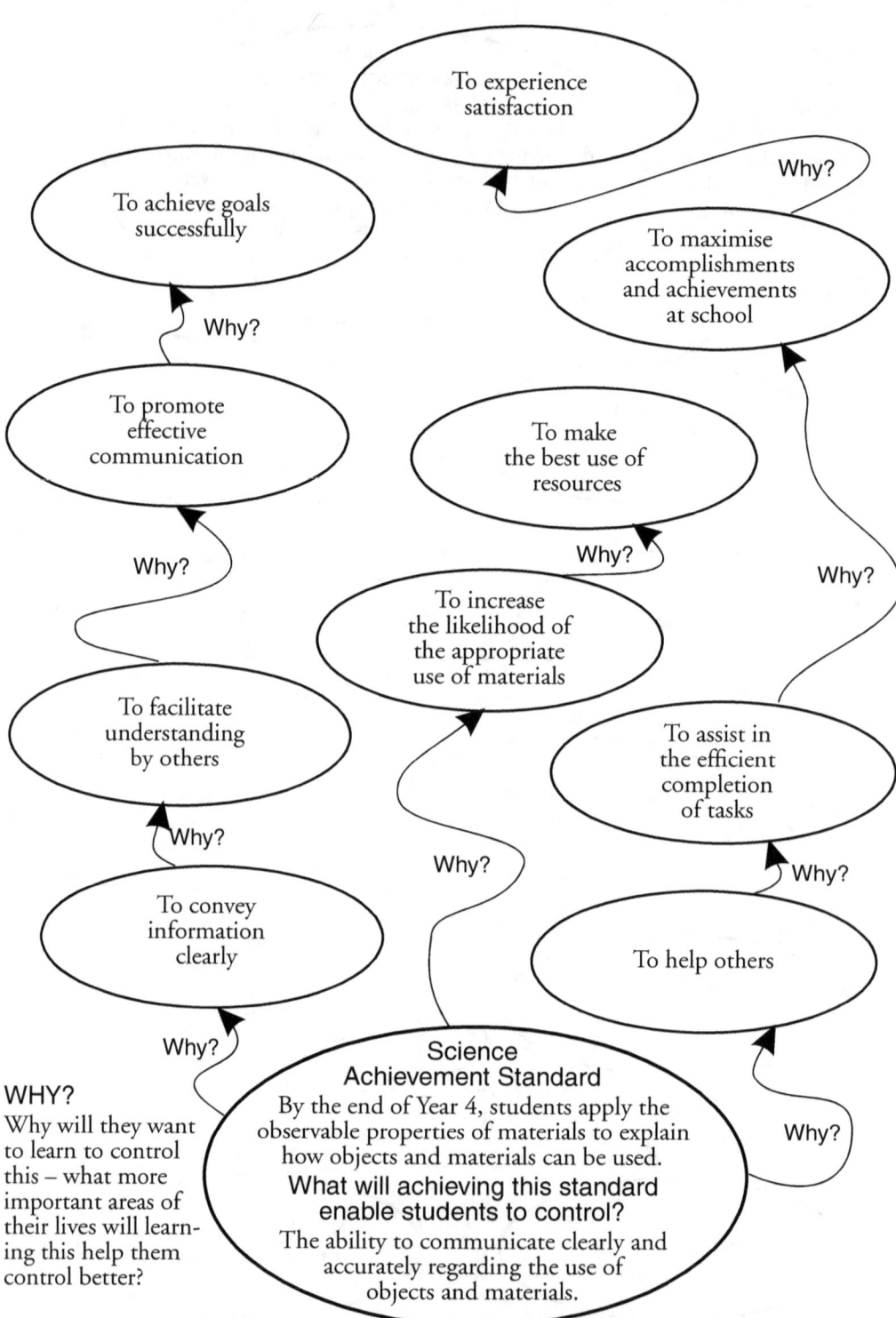

Fitting PCAs Into the Network – Hows

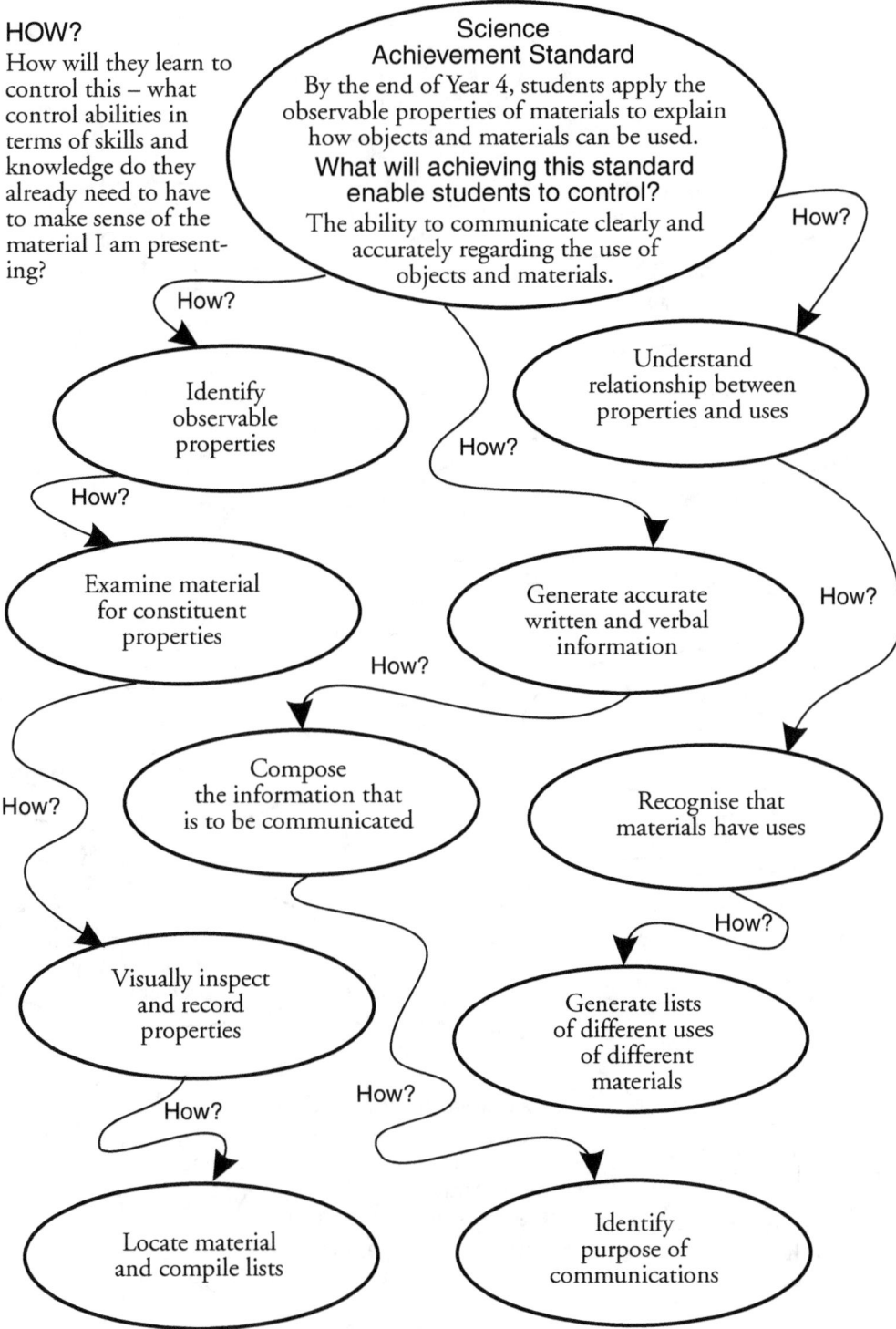

106 Chapter Seven

Fitting PCAs Into the Network – Whys

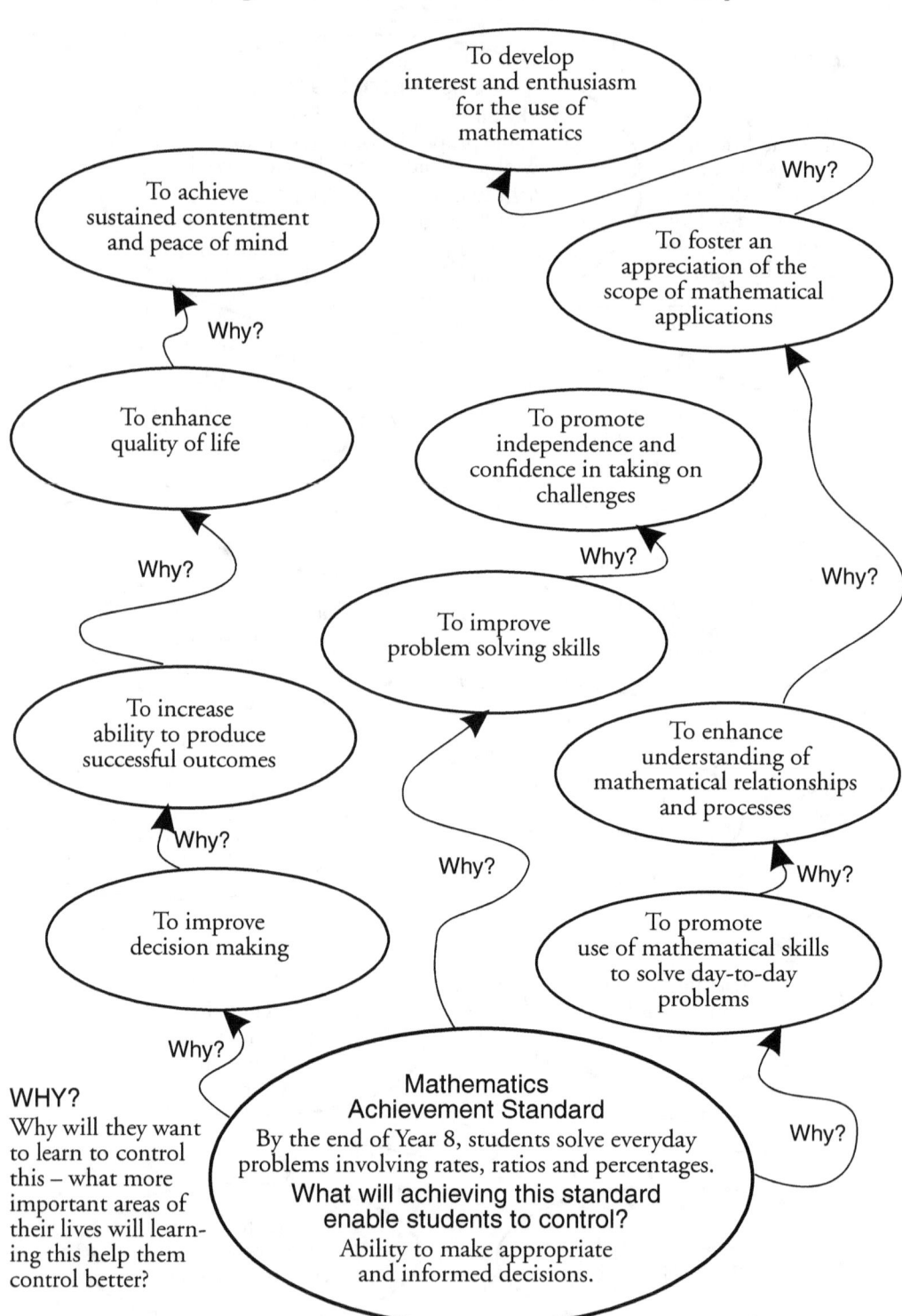

Fitting PCAs Into the Network – Hows

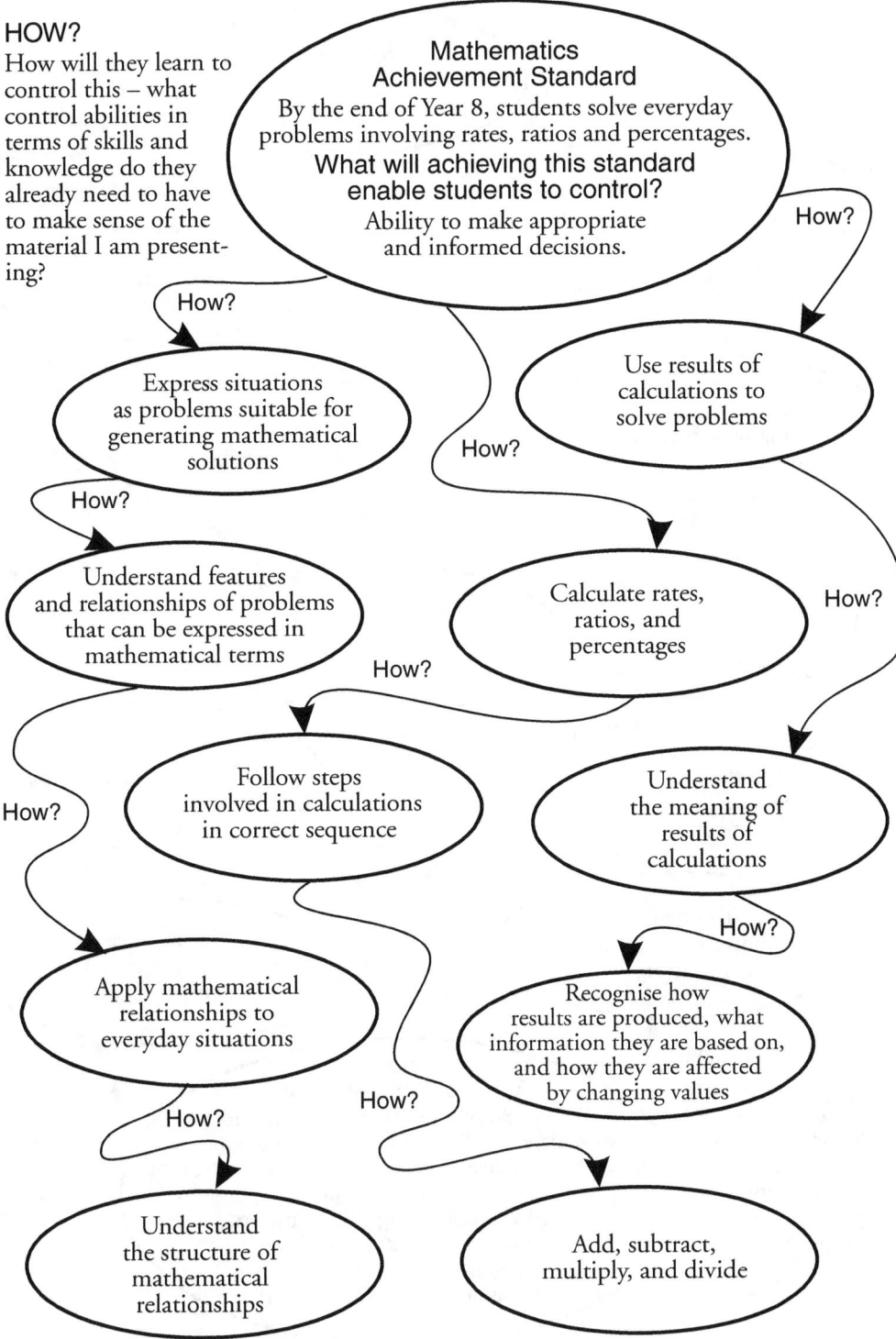

108 Chapter Seven

Fitting PCAs Into the Network – Whys

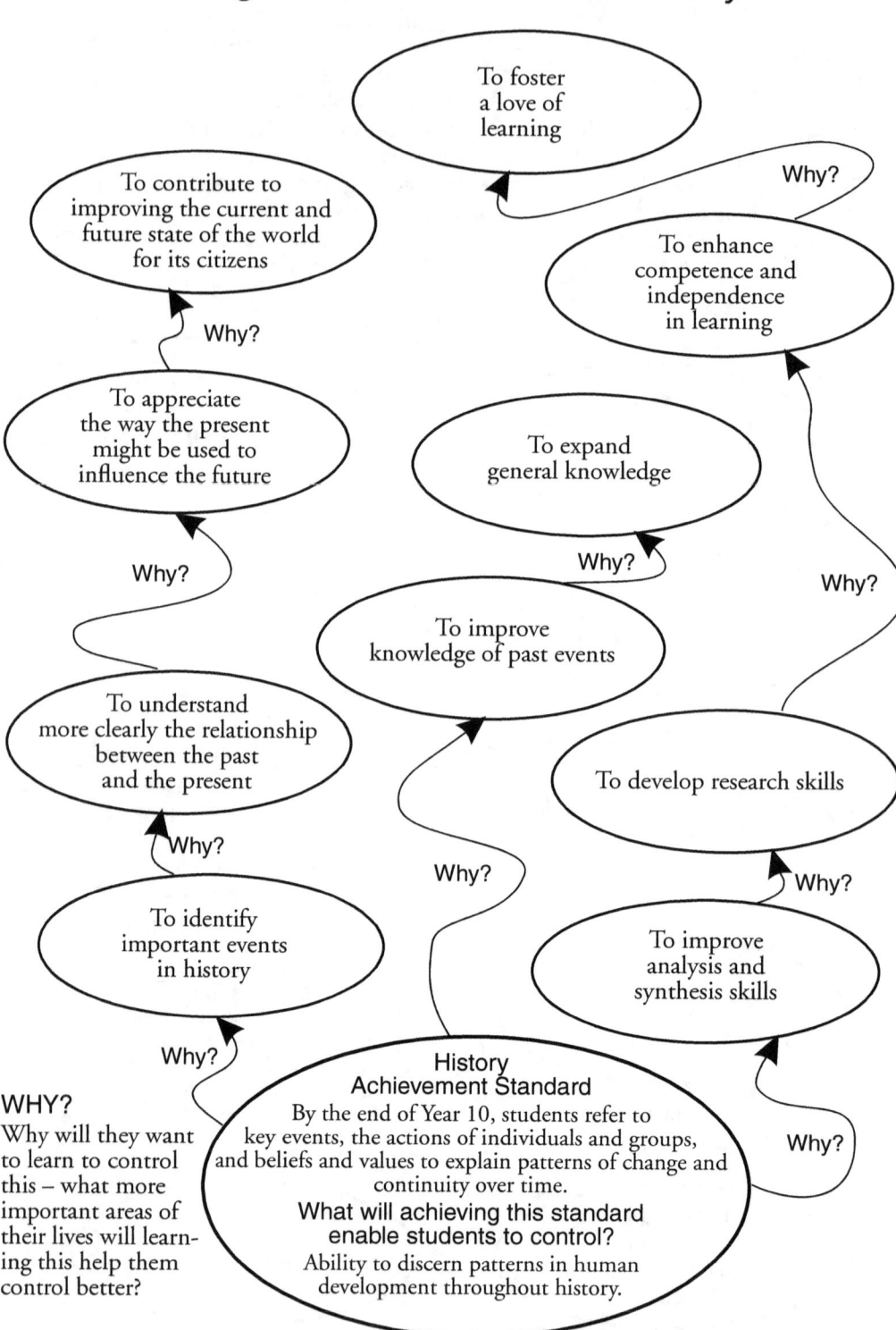

Going About the Business of Teaching 109

Fitting PCAs Into the Network – Hows

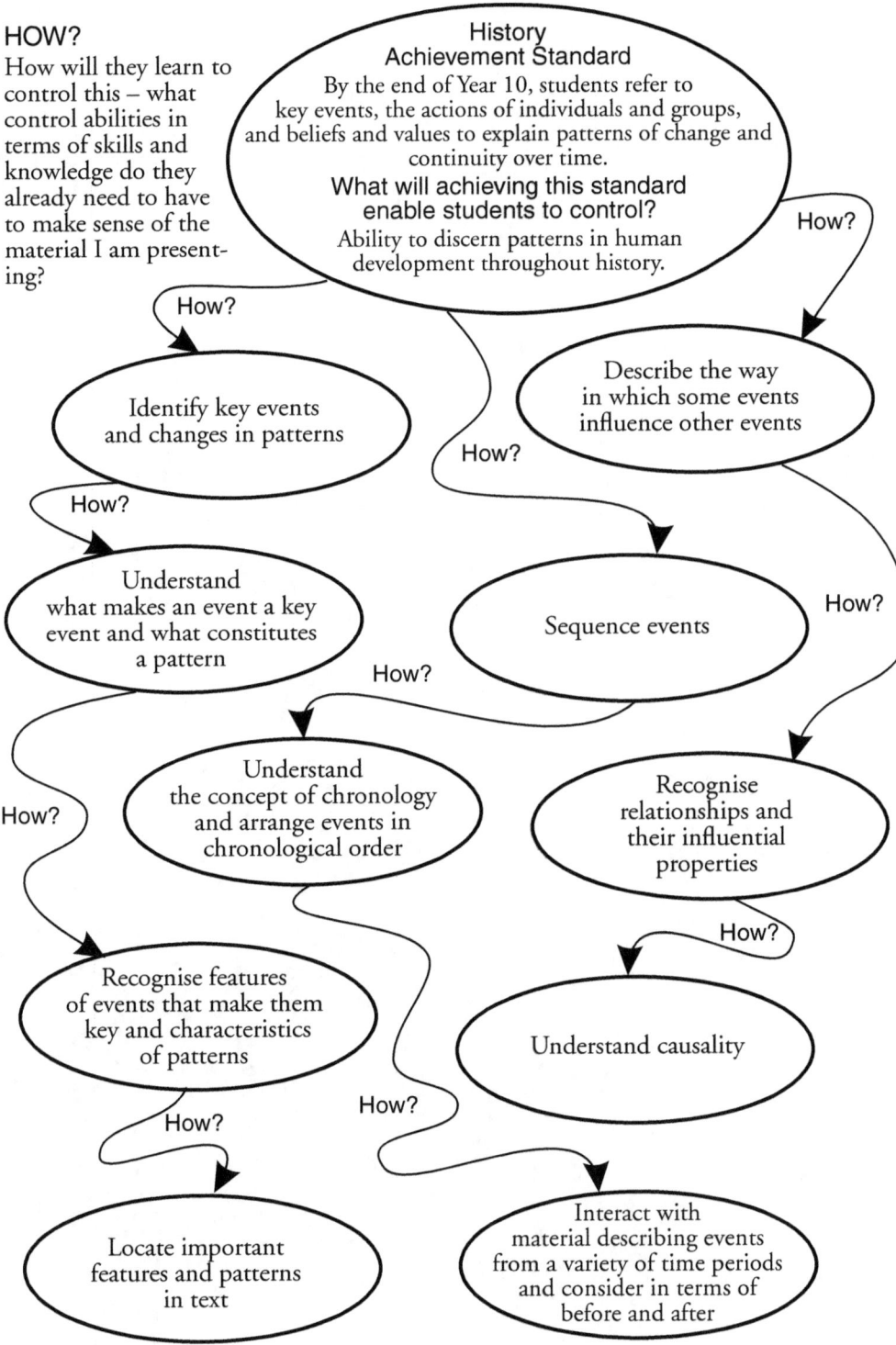

8

Assessment in Educational Settings

*If you read this chapter
you'll understand how to
consider the procedures
and results of testing
and assessment
from a PCA perspective*

Assessment in Educational Settings

The assessment of student learning is an important component of school-based activities. It is interesting to reflect, however, on what assessment is being conducted for. In this chapter I thought it might be useful to begin describing what assessment might be like in a school based on PCA principles. I don't intend this chapter to be an exhaustive account of assessment procedures. Rather, I'll suggest general guidelines and some ideas for assessment methods. As you become comfortable with these ideas, I expect that you will begin to create many more possibilities than I have proposed.

Many of these ideas are based on "Against 'Objective' Tests: A Note on the Epistemology Underlying Current Testing Dogma", especially the section following "The cybernetic alternative", in Hugh Petrie's anthology *Ways of Learning and Knowing; The Epistemology of Education.* See Recommended Reading, page 137.

Perhaps the first thing to be clear about when considering the assessment of PCA learning is just what it is that is being assessed. If learning involves the development and refinement of control abilities, then finding out how well students have learned something entails determining the extent to which they can keep variables in reference states. Essentially then, teachers would investigate whether or not students can counteract the effects of disturbances so that the variables they have been learning to control remain in their just-right (reference) states. Disturbing controlled variables is the main way of assessing learning from a PCA perspective.

From this perspective, assessment is a matter of systematically introducing disturbances to variables that you are presuming students have learned to control, and observing what students do to resist these disturbances. It will also be important then, to consider the context of the assessment. If you apply some disturbances and students do not oppose their effects, it will be important to consider a number of different guesses about what might be happening. The first consideration however, before any ideas about the student's learning ability are explored, should be whether or not the student was interested in opposing the disturbances presented. It will always be the case that some disturbances may be unopposed because the student is interested in other things. Perhaps the student wasn't thrilled about the topic that was being taught and made no effort to acquire the necessary PCA. If you completed the why and how activity sheets before introducing the unit you may even have a sense of who those students might be. Perhaps the student wants to fail the assessment they are undertaking. If they fail this particular assessment it might be the case that they will be able to change subjects or even drop out of school. Initially then, whenever you're trying to make sense of assessment results, it's probably useful to wonder what students were *doing* when they completed the assessment you set for them – that is, what their intentions were.

When a learning problem is suspected it might be fruitful to first ask the question: To whom is the learning problem a problem? What seems like a problem to teachers and parents might not be experienced as a problem by the student. It's only by considering learning from the inside looking out that we can come to a more accurate understanding of what's going on.

Even after considering the issue of students not being interested in opposing the disturbances you presented, it will still be the case that there are many students who are interested in participating in assessment procedures that provide information about how well they are able to control particular variables. The ways that teachers might assess this are many and varied. Again, just like the ships sailing out to sea, a lot of the assessment methods in a PCA school will look the same as the way assessment is conducted in other schools. No doubt there are many ways to provide students with opportunities to counteract disturbances to keep variables in reference states. It's not the methods that will change, therefore, but an understanding of what these methods tell you.

Sometimes humor can be used informally to provide students with opportunities to oppose disturbances. As a preschool teacher I often used this approach. One of the things I was interested in helping students learn at preschool was to assign color labels to the appropriate colors. Obviously the ways that color labels (e.g., "red", "blue", "green", etc.) can be applied to the different hues (e.g., the skin of an apple, the sky, grass) can vary. To communicate with others however there are some commonly accepted conventions about how the labels should be assigned. Some of the opportunities I provided at preschool then were for students to learn to assign labels according to accepted norms. To investigate how well students were able to control this variable (assignment of label to hue) I would occasionally introduce disturbances to students.

Suppose for example that Avery was wearing a blue shirt. I might say "Avery, that's a lovely green shirt you have on". Avery might then say "No, it's not green it's blue." Avery then, had successfully opposed a disturbance I had introduced.

In another situation, however, I might say the same thing to Riley and he might just look at me, smile, and then continue with the activity he was participating in. He has not, in this instance opposed the disturbance I presented. I now have information to consider in the form of some guesses I can make in order to understand what occurred. Seeing Riley turned his head and looked at me I can probably safely assume he actually heard what I said. Is English his first language? Perhaps he didn't understand some of my words. Beyond these preliminaries I need to rule out the idea that Riley was not interested in participating in the conversation I initiated. Perhaps he was playing an enjoyable game with friends and my conversation had interrupted his participation. His smile and shrug then may have been an attempt to oppose the disturbance to game participation rather than to color/label matching. Or maybe Riley believes it is right to agree with the teacher. While he may not agree with my assessment of the color of his shirt he may smile and shrug as a way of keeping another variable – amount of teacher/student agreement – in its just-right state. These hypotheses can perhaps be ruled out more easily if the student has been a willing and voluntary participant in the assessment procedure.

Beyond these initial guesses, however, there are others to consider. If Riley is interested in controlling his perception of color/label matching I would wonder about his apparent inability to oppose my disturbance. Perhaps he did not clearly hear what I said. Perhaps he is color blind. Perhaps at this stage he only has references for red, blue, and yellow. Perhaps he doesn't know how to disagree with me in order to make the color match be right.

All of these guesses would give me information for future programming (of learning opportunities – not Riley!) and further opportunities for Riley. I might introduce games and other activities that have a color/label matching component. When we're cooking, I might ask Riley to bring me the red plate to put our freshly baked biscuits on. By observing Riley's actions in these activities I will be able to gather additional information to assist me in confirming or dispelling the guesses I've made. The activities will also provide Riley with opportunities to build the PCA necessary to successfully match colors with labels if that is what he wants to do.

Sometimes testing can happen in another way. Suppose I asked Madeline to go and get me the yellow cup. At first she might come back with the green cup which I point out to her and ask her for the yellow one. She comes back with the blue cup this time and then the red cup and then the purple cup and then the blue cup again and … If Madeline *never once* brings me the yellow cup (and there's actually a yellow cup on the shelf) you might once again wonder about what she is controlling. In this scenario, the simplest explanation would be that Madeline does indeed know which cup is yellow, since you would expect just by a sheer fluke she would grab the yellow cup eventually if she really didn't know which color was which. If all the cups get picked except the yellow one you might suspect that Madeline was *avoiding* the yellow cup. Perhaps she is enjoying her interaction with you and doesn't want it to end, which is what would happen if she brought over the cup of the right color. Sometimes looking at behavior in a slightly different way can be illuminating.

While these examples have been from a preschool setting the same principles apply regardless of the age of the student or the educational opportunities being provided. At all times, what the teacher is assessing is the student's ability to counteract the effect of disturbances in order to keep variables in their just-right states. Questions with multiple choice solutions are another way of introducing disturbances for students to oppose. An item such as this gives students the opportunity to oppose disturbances by selecting the correct response:

The order of planets in the solar system is:

a) Mars, Jupiter, Venus, Earth, Pluto, Mercury, Saturn, Uranus, Neptune

b) Mercury, Venus, Earth, Mars, Jupiter, Saturn, Uranus, Neptune, Pluto

c) Earth, Pluto, Saturn, Mercury, Mars, Uranus, Neptune, Venus, Jupiter

d) Jupiter, Mars, Pluto, Mercury, Saturn, Earth, Uranus, Mars, Venus

True/False and Yes/No items such as this provide the same opportunities with more limited options:

Tadpoles are young lizards.   TRUE   FALSE

Other assessment methods could be short-answer and essay responses to various problems. These methods give students more flexible and creative ways of expressing their resistance to disturbances. Also, demonstrations such as matching, solving problems, building models, or presenting information orally give students rich opportunities to exercise control over variables in assessment forums. Interviews allow teachers to interject a number of disturbances and observe the student's responses to them.

At all times, the focus should be on the student's control of perceptual variables. What is being assessed is a student's ability to control. How well established is their PCA with respect to this subject matter? How well can they oppose disturbances to keep things just right? Can they only oppose very large disturbances or are they alert to subtle ones too? The information obtained from assessment methods will give you important clues about the planning of future learning opportunities. When students' responses are obtained, it might be useful to consider their perspective when making guesses about their ability to control the variable in question. If you've ruled out some of the preliminary and contextual information you could assume the students were trying to give you the correct answer. For each individual student then you might consider the question:

What might the student's understanding be to endorse this as the correct response?

That is, if students do consider that their responses had successfully opposed the disturbance you introduced, how must they understand the situation? This question might once again give you useful guidelines for future learning opportunities. The students might have developed just-rights that are different from the one you have in mind. They may perceive the variable slightly differently, or perhaps the comparisons they make between their perception and their reference are different from what you expect. All of these possibilities would be useful to explore if you are to help them control more successfully.

This concept of assessment subsumes all forms of assessment in educational settings, from routine classroom assessments to the assessment of learning and behavioral problems. In PCA schools, traditional diagnostic labels would not be so helpful. Labels such as Attention Deficit Disorder, Asperger's Disorder, Tourette's Syndrome, Mildly Intellectually Disabled and Developmentally Delayed are all constructed from an understanding of behavior that is very different from the PCA understanding. These labels are essentially categories of different kinds of actions or behaviors. If a student acts in a particular way for a certain period of time they may be assigned one of these labels depending on the behaviors that are observed.

In a PCA world, however, it is not the behaviors that are of interest, but rather what experiences or outcomes these behaviors are creating and maintaining for the individual involved. The behavior is just the person's way to oppose environmental disturbances. When people's behavior seems erratic therefore, one of the first things to conclude is that the environment probably seems erratic from their point of view. Taking time to investigate what it is the person is controlling (by going on a hunt for controlled variables) will do much to ensure that the assessments the student is involved in are meaningful for them.

This is not to say that problems don't occur. Problems can arise in numerous ways for PCAs. The student may have a problem with the information that is coming in. Some students may have perceptions that are very different from how other people perceive the same experience. This simple explanation may account for phenomena such as color blindness or tunnel vision. Perhaps children who might attract a diagnosis of autism have perceptions that are very much magnified compared to other people, so that they receive much more sensory input than other people do. Similar problems can occur where the comparison is made and also where the error signal goes. If problems were assessed according to the PCA design, interventions could be introduced to help the students more effectively control the variables that are important to them.

Sometimes a PCA is functioning appropriately but the person may have a different reference for what they should experience. Burgess might steal, for example, not because he dislikes his teachers or his peers, but he may have a different reference level with respect to personal property than other students. Perhaps his experiences so far have been about collective ownership of belongings. Students from different schools may have different just-rights with respect to the correct sequence of procedures for long division or the correct formation of letters when writing. These students have nothing wrong with their PCAs, the just-rights that they previously learned to control in coordination with others are different from those that are controlled at the school they now attend. These students then, could be provided with opportunities to adopt new reference levels for their already functioning PCAs.

The way information is gathered will depend on the phenomenon under scrutiny. From a PCA perspective it is understood that people control their experiences. Assessment procedures, therefore, that are commensurate with this approach would be designed to assess how efficiently students can oppose those things that disturb some variable aspect of their perceptual environment. All forms of assessment would be approached in this way. What happens after the results of the assessment have come in would depend on how the results are understood. Any interventions or treatments that are offered as a consequence of the assessment will be concerned with helping students establish better control over some aspect of their environment.

Assessment Form

PRE-ASSESSMENT

Control of what variable am I interested in assessing?
  The procedure for calculating the mean of a set of numbers

Is the student I am assessing a willing participant in the assessment process?   (YES)   NO

What is the reference state for this variable?
  Three steps: count how many numbers there are; add up all the numbers; divide the total by how many there are

What are some ways I can disturb this variable?
  Suggest that the student might actually be calculating the median. Suggest that the student add the numbers up first and then count how many there are (this shouldn't matter to the student). Suggest that there might be a mistake because the answer that was calculated is not a whole number. Ask the student how they will deal with numbers that are the same in the data set (that shouldn't matter although it might for the median or the mode) or what they will do if the total amount of data is an even number.

What should I observe from the student if they are able to oppose the disturbances?
  They'll complete the procedure efficiently. They won't be bothered by the order in which they count the numbers and add them up and they also won't be bothered by numbers that are the same or if the answer contains decimal numbers.

POST-ASSESSMENT

What did I observe from the student?
  Easily managed the situation of counting the numbers and adding them up in either order. Hesitated for a little while when considering repeats of the same number and also how they would handle an even number for the total number in the data set.

What hypotheses seem reasonable in explaining my observations?
  Still not completely confident in differentiating procedure for calculating mean from procedure for calculating median or mode.

What opportunities can I now provide this student to help them improve their ability to control this variable?
  More practice with calculating all three. Activities where they get a data set and they have to predict what the mean, median, and mode will be and then they go ahead and calculate them. Have them teach one of the other students or a student from a younger grade how to calculate them.

Note: For blank copies of this and other forms, see page 145 in this book.

Classroom Procedures

If you read this chapter you'll find some ways to promote the PCAness of your classroom

Classroom Procedures

Now that we've discussed the ins and outs of learning from a PCA perspective I thought it might be a useful way to finish off the book by discussing more specifically the kinds of things that teachers might do on a day-to-day basis to adopt PCA practices. While reading this chapter it may be useful to revisit some of the earlier topics we've discussed. It will be important to keep in mind, for example, that a teacher's role, as I'm discussing it here, is to be educationally useful to students and that the core business of schools is to help students learn to control certain variable aspects of the different environments they move in and out of. The procedures I describe here are not the only ones possible, but I'm introducing them to help you in your pursuit of being more educationally useful to your students.

Activities such as classroom discussions and morning meetings are a way for teachers to provide students with the experience of negotiation and compromise that we discussed earlier. The topics that could be explored in classroom discussions are practically limitless. In fact the content of what is discussed is not as important as providing students with an experience of conversing in a social group and encountering all that goes with an experience of this kind – taking turns to talk, being disagreed with, hearing opinions different from your own, and so on.

You could begin with a topic in mind or even ask the students to nominate a topic. Once the topic has been decided, your goal would be to provide students with an opportunity to present their ideas. You can do this by asking the students questions about what is being discussed. Open-ended questions that invite explanation and elaboration are better than closed-ended questions that only require a "yes" or "no" response. Also, disagreement between students should be encouraged. When students express different opinions you should take the time to ask each student about the other's opinion. Asking for opinions from other students is useful too. Structuring the discussions in this way can let students know that it is not important to agree with other people all the time. It is important to consider the way that you disagree with others, however, if you wish to do what you can to maintain a relationship with that person. Obviously, the extent to which you pursue and explore disagreements will depend on the age and capabilities of your students but, with that proviso, students are probably never too young to start this sort of thing.

Classroom discussions can be used for a variety of purposes. They are very useful vehicles for resolving classroom problems such as difficulties with routines or social problems such as teasing. Also, they can be used at the start of a unit of work to ascertain what students already know about the topic to be introduced. They can also be used to discuss various issues related to social living. Topics such as "trust", "respect", and "cooperation" can all be explored in classroom discussions. During these discussions the teacher would be interested in providing students with opportunities to explain their own ideas about these topics. That is, students might explain what they understand cooperation to be, how important it is to them, why they think it's important, and what their own personal standard of cooperation is. These discussions are a useful way of maximizing the extent to which negotiation occurs in the classroom.

Discussions can occur as often as you want to conduct them. It would not be unrealistic to have one discussion per day. The start of the day, for example, could begin with a discussion about what was to be covered for the day and how the class might go about completing the tasks. Any problems that occurred throughout the day could be resolved in the forum of a classroom discussion. Once discussions have become an established part of classroom routines, students may even be able to organize smaller scale discussions on their own whenever they need to resolve difficulties between them.

In Secondary School classes, perhaps one lesson each week could be devoted to these kinds of discussions. That's a big chunk out of your teaching time, but the benefits that can be gained in understanding your students may well make up for any time lost in formal instruction. You might find that allocating this time each week actually improves the efficiency and congeniality of the other classes in the week.

Just as discussions would be an established part of classroom routines in a PCA school, so too would planning. Planning essentially involves teachers assisting students to achieve goals through a formal structured process. The particular goals that students nominate are not as important as learning the process of making plans to create intended experiences. The form at the end of this chapter may help teachers structure this process with students.

When people are understood as beings of a PCA nature then focusing on goals becomes a no-brainer. In the PCA design, goals are the references or just-right states that are so important to the control process. Our actions at any point in time are always the result of the combined effects of our goals and the disturbing forces in the environment. Paying attention to goals then is an important way of helping people get what they want.

Planning can be a way of enabling students to create and maintain the just-rights that are important to them. Perhaps students could nominate something they would like to work on for the school term. The goal could well be academic, but it may be social as well. Students might plan to achieve a particular grade or to accomplish a certain amount of work. They might also plan to make new friends or to solve conflicts in socially appropriate ways. Once the term goal has been identified, students might then set weekly goals that will help them achieve the term goal. At the end of every day then, the teacher would provide time for the students to evaluate their weekly goal. When the week is over the students will set a new goal for the next week that will move them closer to the realization of their term goal. This kind of regular goal setting, evaluating, and planning is exactly the kind of skill that will help students succeed at university and in jobs they move into. It will also help them build the relationships they want and pursue the futures they daydream about.

The why and how questions that we've already discussed are especially useful here. There's a lot of fun that can be had with these little tricksters. Perhaps it would be interesting to make these questions the topic of a morning meeting or classroom discussion. You could start with a question such as "Why do you come to school?" and take it from there. It might be really interesting for you as well as your students to hear the variety of answers to that question and also to follow the different paths that the why questions invite your students to take.

When students identify a goal that they want to work on, they might find it helpful to gain a sense of where this particular goal fits within their network of PCAs. For example, suppose Grace sets a goal at the beginning of the term "to complete set homework every night". You might ask "why do you want to complete set homework every night". She might answer "to get good grades". You could continue with "why do you want to get good grades". Grace's answer to this might be "to go to university". So, in only two questions you have helped Grace identify a more important goal that "completing set homework every night" will help achieve. Whenever goals are becoming dreary it can help to check out whether the higher goal is still there or whether something important has changed. Notice too, that Caleb might answer "to avoid lunchtime detentions" in answer to your question of "why do you want to complete set homework every night". In answer to "why do you want to avoid lunch time detentions" he might say "to spend time with my friends". Now there are two very different purposes – going to university, and spending time with friends – for which completing homework is being used. Neither of these goals is right or wrong, but the information will be helpful in understanding your students and learning how they can be helped and supported more effectively. It doesn't matter, therefore, if students provide different answers to your question – in fact that should be expected. It's quite wonderful, actually, to gain even a little glimpse of some of the ways that other people's PCA networks are put together.

"How" questions can follow similar divergent paths. "How are you going to complete set homework every night" might be answered with "I'll set aside an hour before dinner every night" and then "I'll ask my mom and dad to remind me" by Arianna. Diego, however, might answer "I'll stay at school for an extra hour in the afternoon" and then "I'll ask my mom to pick me up after she does the shopping instead of before".

The answers, in fact, aren't as important as providing students with a process of getting to know themselves a little better. "Why" questions will help them become more aware of the goals that are important to them and "how" questions will help them identify the ways that they can achieve these goals. This process is primarily for them, so you don't have to be concerned about whether or not they're telling you the truth or giving you the correct answer.

Planning should be a routine procedure of PCA classrooms. The activity we've just been through is quite a formal way of teaching students planning. Planning can also be done informally on a continual basis during classroom activities. At the beginning of a lesson, for example, teachers could explain to students what will be covered in the following lesson and then ask students to nominate what experiences or outcomes they will be controlling in the lesson. Also, at the beginning of a new unit of work the teacher could explain what will be covered and what the assessment will be. Students then could be encouraged to nominate the academic standard (their just-right) that they will be controlling throughout the forthcoming unit. Helping students learn to self-evaluate will be extremely useful for them as they undertake the acquisition of new control abilities.

Just as planning can become routine, so can evaluating the plans. By asking the students to think about their goals from time to time you will be helping to demonstrate how important this activity is. You could, for example, ask students at random times to rate on a scale from 1 (not at all) to 10 (a lot) how close they are to their goal at that moment. You could also set your own goals and make plans for how you will achieve them, which will be another way of demonstrating the usefulness of this activity.

As with all other activities, even though planning and classroom discussions are regarded as being crucial to fostering harmonious relationships and promoting learning and achievement through the acknowledgement of control processes, they should also be considered to be voluntary. It would be completely antithetical to PCA principles to attempt to direct or force a student to participate in something that they would otherwise not do. Planning and classroom discussions are offered as opportunities for students to gain certain experiences. It is a teacher's responsibility to continually offer the opportunity and to maintain an invitational attitude towards student participation. It is not the teacher's responsibility to introduce incentives or penalties to promote student participation.

The final procedure to be discussed is that of questioning. In PCA classrooms teachers would minimize the extent to which they tell students what to do and maximize the extent to which they ask students questions. When questions are asked of students, you have a greater chance of accessing the students' perceptions of the world than when you instruct or direct. Continually asking questions will allow you to gain a greater understanding of what is important to the students and how they are making sense of the classroom experience.

To be sure, it is sometimes necessary to provide instruction and information to students. There would not seem to be very much educational value in asking "What do you think a good name would be for the long side of a right angled triangle?" when you are wanting students to learn about the hypotenuse. It is likely to be the case, however, that the balance between how much time is spent asking questions and how much time is spent directing or giving instructions could be shifted. Looking for ways to maximize question asking and changing directions into questions will help you be more educationally useful to students.

The bottom line when PCAing a school is to structure the environment such that everyone has the opportunity to control their own experiences with a minimum of interference – that is, so that degrees of freedom are maximized. Within schooling environments, as with any other environment, it will not be possible to control everything. Throughout this book I have described how you might best assist students to control what it is appropriate to control in school settings. I have also suggested what teachers might do when students are not interested in controlling what is currently on offer. These PCA ideas, and the theory behind them (PCT), offer teachers the opportunity to understand their role in a way that they may not have considered before. This new understanding may help you to control your own perceptions more effectively and, perhaps surprisingly, may help you to assist students to do the same.

Term Planning Sheet

My goal for this term is:
Improve my standard in completing book reviews.

Achieving this goal is important to me because:
I need to improve my overall grade in English.

To know that I have achieved this goal I will need to:
Have finished reading the book by ½ way through the term and get a first draft completed in the 4th last week of term.

How close am I to achieving my goal?

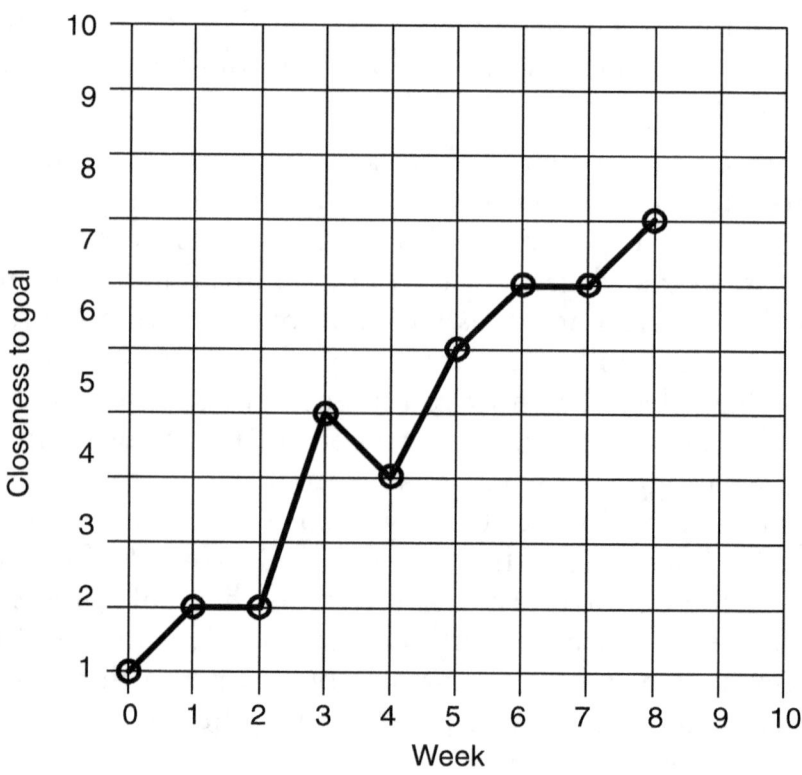

Note: For blank copies of this and other forms, see page 145 in this book.

Weekly Planning Sheet

My goal for this week:
Read 3 chapters and make notes of how the characters are described.

It will help me achieve my term goal because:
It will help get the book read and the review will be easier to write if I've made notes.

I will get more of what I want in class if I achieve this goal because:
I'll be able to participate in the class discussions when they're talking about the novel because I'll know what they're talking about and that will help me write a better review too.

I will know I'm achieving my goal when:
I'm reading the book.
I'll need to spend at least 40 minutes every night reading.

Monday
need to improve					OK			doing great	
1	2	3	4	5	6	7	(8)	9	10

Tuesday
need to improve					OK			doing great	
1	2	3	4	(5)	6	7	8	9	10

Wednesday
need to improve					OK			doing great	
1	2	3	4	5	(6)	7	8	9	10

Thursday
need to improve					OK			doing great	
1	2	3	4	5	6	7	(8)	9	10

Friday
need to improve					OK			doing great	
1	2	3	4	5	6	7	8	(9)	10

My goal for next week is:
Read the next three chapters. Ask the teacher if my notes are OK – am I writing down the right things?

Useful Websites

*If you visit these sites
you can learn much,
much more about PCT*

www.livingcontrolsystems.com

The publisher's website features books and introductions to PCT, plus tutorials and simulation programs you can run on Windows.

www.pctweb.org

This well developed website is maintained by Dr Warren Mansell from the University of Manchester as an international resource for the dissemination of PCT.

www.mindreadings.com

Rick Marken's website features books, articles and demonstrations you run using your Internet browser.

www.iapct.org

Website for the International Association for Perceptual Control Theory, IAPCT.

recommended reading

*Books you should curl up with
on a cold Winter's night
(or anytime at all really)*

Books in order by author and publication date, except for Cziko.

Publishers

Benchmark: Bloomfield, NJ: Benchmark Publications.
LCSP: Menlo Park CA: Living Control Systems Publishing.
Kiddy World: Arnhem, The Netherlands: Kiddy World Promotions B.V.
MIT: Cambridge MA: MIT Press.
New View: Chapel Hill, N.C.: New View Publications.
Routledge: Routledge / Taylor & Francis.

Books by LCSP can be downloaded at the publisher's website.

Carey, Timothy A. (2006). *The Method of Levels: How to do Psychotherapy Without Getting in the Way.* LCSP.

Tim Carey is the peerless expert on and practitioner of the Method Of Levels (MOL), based on the hierarchical structure of PCT. While working for Scotland's National Health Service he used this approach exclusively with his primary care patients. Some of his colleagues learned MOL from Tim and used it too. MOL achieved a new level of service efficiency as evidenced by the fact that the waiting list went from 15 months when he arrived to less than one month five years later.

Carey, Timothy A. (2008). *Hold That Thought! Two Steps to Effective Counseling and Psychotherapy With the Method of Levels.* New View.

Believing that people with psychological problems get themselves better, Carey introduces readers to the Method of Levels, an approach to psychotherapy based on PCT.

Carey's lighthearted style does not obscure his message: that people can change only themselves, and do not need prescriptive solutions from psychotherapists. With lots of examples, Carey shows readers how to find a new perspective on their conflict and ultimately resolve it.

Mansell, Warren, Carey, Timothy A., and Tai, Sara (Dec. 2012). *A Transdiagnostic Approach to CBT using Method of Levels Therapy.* Routledge.

This innovative volume will be essential reading for freshly minted as well as experienced Cognitive Behavior Therapists (CBT) who wish to work using a transdiagnostic approach. Its core principles also apply to counselling, psychotherapy and a range of helping professions. Its accessible explanation of Perceptual Control Theory and its application to real world problems also makes a useful resource for undergraduates, graduates and researchers in psychology.

Cziko, Gary (1995). *Without Miracles: Universal Selection Theory and the Second Darwinian Revolution.* MIT.

Cziko, Gary (2000). *The Things We Do: Using the Lessons of Bernard and Darwin to Understand the What, How, and Why of Our Behavior.* MIT.

The inside flap of *The Things We Do* (Complete)

The remarkable achievements that modern science has made in physics, chemistry, biology, medicine, and engineering contrast sharply with our limited knowledge of the human mind and behavior. A major reason for this slow progress, claims Gary Cziko, is that with few exceptions, behavioral and cognitive scientists continue to apply a Newtonian-inspired view of animate behavior as an organisms output determined by environmental input. This one-way cause-effect approach ignores the important findings of two major nineteenth-century biologists, French psychologist Claude Bernard and English naturalist Charles Darwin.

Approaching living organisms as purposeful systems that behave in order to control their perceptions of the external environment provides a new perspective for understanding what, how, and why living beings, including humans, do what they do.

Cziko examines in particular perceptual control theory, which has its roots in Bernard's work on the self-regulating nature of living organisms and in the work of engineers who developed the field of cybernetics during and after World War II. He also shows how our evolutionary past together with Darwinian processes currently occurring within our bodies, such as the evolution of new brain connections, provides insights into the immediate and ultimate causes of behavior.

Writing in an accessible style, Cziko shows how the lessons of Bernard and Darwin, updated with the best of current scientific knowledge, can provide solutions to certain long-standing theoretical and practical problems in behavioral science and enable us to develop new methods and topics for research.

Gary Cziko is Professor and AT&T Technology Fellow in the Department of Educational Psychology at the University of Illinois, Urbana-Champaign. He is the author of *Without Miracles* (MIT Press, 1995).

Petrie Hugh G. (2012). *Ways of Learning and Knowing.* LCSP.

For most of his career, Hugh was way ahead of his time. His papers in this volume still are. The role of the evolutionary process of blind variation and selective retention in all knowledge processes and the understanding of behavior as the control of perception are still mostly unknown in mainstream educational research, theory and philosophy. These perspectives, combined with Hugh's analytical skills and accessible writing, lead to some radical (and radically useful) implications for our understanding of the process of knowledge growth and the practice of education.

— Gary Cziko

Powers, William T. (1973). *Behavior: The Control of Perception* Second edition (2005). Revised and expanded. Benchmark.

Powers' manuscript, *Behavior: The Control of Perception*, is among the most exciting I have read in some time. The problems are of vast importance, and not only to psychologists; the achieved synthesis is thoroughly original; and the presentation is often convincing and almost invariably suggestive. I shall be watching with interest what happens to research in the directions to which Powers points.

— Thomas S. Kuhn

Powers, William T. (1989). *Living Control Systems: Selected Papers of William T. Powers*. Benchmark.

Powers, William T. (1992). *Living Control Systems II: Selected Papers of William T. Powers*. Benchmark.

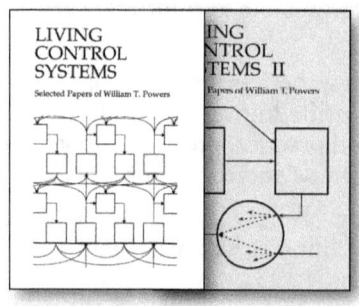

Some of the best science is done by people who refuse to take the obvious for granted. Copernicus didn't take the sun's daily trek across the sky for granted, and Einstein didn't take the regular tick of time for granted, and William T. Powers didn't take the appearance of behavior for granted.

— Richard S. Marken

Recommended Reading 141

Powers, William T. (1998). *Making Sense of Behavior: The Meaning of Control.* Benchmark.

This is the first book on PCT written for "the rest of us." Powers describes in a relaxed, easy-to-read style the fundamentals of this revolutionary theory of the behavior of living organisms—in particular, human beings.

This book is for anyone interested in how our systems work and how people interact and why. For researchers new to PCT, a comprehensive reference points to further studies, demonstrations and applications.

Powers, William T. (2008). *Living control systems III: The Fact of Control.* Benchmark.

... A unique feature of the book is the accompanying computer programs where Powers 'puts his models where his mouth is,' graphically demonstrating how negative feedback control systems can account for a wide range of goal-oriented behavior. This book is required reading (and computing) for anyone seeking a deep understanding of the behavior of living organisms.

— Gary Cziko

Powers, William T. (Creator). (2016 version).
Perceptual Control Theory; An Overview of the Third Grand Theory in Psychology—Introductions, Readings, and Resources. LCSP.

This *"Book of Readingss"* provides a sampling of the literature on Perceptual Control Theory, the science and applications to date.

34 papers cover subjects such as Science, Origin, Comparisons, Demonstrations, Therapy, and Dogma.

Chapters and samples from 24 books on PCT.

Free PDF file at the LCSP website along with all other books published by LCSP.

Powers, William T. and Runkel, Philip J. (2011)
Dialogue Concerning the Two Chief Approaches to a Science of Life: Word Pictures and Correlations versus Working Models. LCSP.

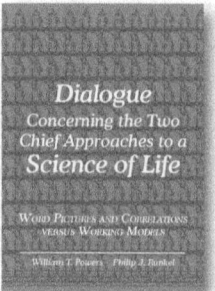

This book holds more than 500 pages of tightly focused, original correspondence between two lucid gentlemen—the creator of PCT, William T. (Bill) Powers, and Philip J. (Phil) Runkel. The significance of the correspondence lies in the subject matter, Perceptual Control Theory (PCT). The preface and Part II provide
—a brief introduction to PCT (p. 509)
—notes regarding PCT and scientific revolutions
—a guide to resources for your study of PCT

Roy, Shelley A.W. (2008). *A People Primer: The Nature of Living Systems.* New View.

What a blast of a book! Shelley Roy obviously has a deep and clear understanding of Perceptual Control Theory, and her style of presentation shows respect for the intelligence of the reader while at the same time making sure that her message gets across. Shelley successfully suppresses the writer's ego and never condescends—a very nice combination.

— William T. Powers

Runkel, Philip J. (1990). *Casting Nets and Testing Specimens.* Second edition (2007). Revised and updated. LCSP.

A major contribution to the study and practice of socio-psychological research. Runkel's prescriptions understood and followed would revolutionize the behavioral sciences. ... Runkel shows what statistical studies of groups of people, which he calls the method of relative frequencies or "casting nets" can do and what it cannot do: tell anything specific about the nature of individuals. Runkel shows how the scientific study of the individual can get done, what he calls "the method of specimens."

— Bruce I. Kodish

Runkel, Philip J. (2003). *People as Living Things: The Psychology of Perceptual Control.* LCSP.

Runkel has written a book ... which is at one and the same time: a text book for graduate and undergraduate psychology; an introduction to perceptual control theory (PCT) for the general reader; a paean to William Powers and his achievement—PCT; a memoir about his (Runkel's) exposure to PCT; and an integration of the research and theoretical work on PCT for those familiar with the theory. In my opinion, he succeeds in all these tasks....

— Len Lansky's complete review:
tinyurl.com/lansky-runkel

van de Rijt, Hetty, and Plooij, Frans (2010). *The Wonder Weeks: How to stimulate your baby's mental development and help him turn his 10 predictable, great, fussy phases into magical leaps forward.* Kiddy World.

The Dutch title for *The Wonder Weeks* can be translated as *Wow, I Am Growing.* Since the original Dutch version was published in 1992, it has sold more than 550,000 copies —in a country of 17 million, one 20th that of the U.S.

This book shows how and when the levels of perception outlined by Hierarchical PCT develop in human infants. The English edition enjoys excellent reviews at Amazon and numerous comments by mommy-bloggers, saying that the predictions about the timing and nature of infant mental development in the first 20 months are right on.

Papers recommended – download and enjoy
These and many more at www.livingcontrolsystems.com

Powers, William T. (2009).   *PCT in 11 Steps.*
Powers, William T. (2009).   *Reorganization and MOL.*
Soldani, James (1989).   *Effective Personnel Management: An Application of Control Theory.*
Soldani, James (2010).   *How I Applied PCT to Get Results.*

blank forms

*Copy forms from the following pages
or download A4 / letter size pdfs
from www.livingcontrolsystems.com
under web page for this book*

Hunting for Controlled Variables

What's going on?	Student's actions	Your best guess about the student's just-right	Checking it out	What happens?

This form is featured on page 64

Assessment Form

PRE-ASSESSMENT

Control of what variable am I interested in assessing?

Is the student I am assessing a willing participant in the assessment process?   **YES**   **NO**

What is the reference state for this variable?

What are some ways I can disturb this variable?

What should I observe from the student if they are able to oppose the disturbances?

POST-ASSESSMENT

What did I observe from the student?

What hypotheses seem reasonable in explaining my observations?

What opportunities can I now provide this student to help them improve their ability to control this variable?

This form is featured on page 121

Increasing Experiences of Negotiation

Date: _____

PRENEGOTIATION

How much negotiation occurs between my students and me? (circle one)

    a little   some   a lot
  1   2   3   4   5   6   7   8   9   10

How much negotiation would my students say occurs in our class?

    a little   some   a lot
  1   2   3   4   5   6   7   8   9   10

How much negotiation would I like to occur between my students and me?

    a little   some   a lot
  1   2   3   4   5   6   7   8   9   10

What aspects of the school and classroom program are nonnegotiable?
1. _____
2. _____
3. _____
4. _____
5. _____

What aspects of the school and classroom program can be negotiated?
1. _____
2. _____
3. _____
4. _____
5. _____

What will I negotiate first?
_____

Do I have an outcome I would prefer?   YES   NO

If yes, what is my preference?
_____
_____

This form is featured on pages 84-85

What will I do if students suggest things I'm not entirely happy with?

When will I conduct the negotiation?

How long do I expect the negotiation to take?

What sorts of questions will I ask during the negotiation?

POSTNEGOTIATION

My overall impression was that the negotiation session was:

   unsuccessful   somewhat successful   very successful

Generally, I was happy with the way I:

To improve future negotiations I could:

The next thing I will negotiate is:

I will conduct this negotiation on:

PCT-Based Lesson Plan

My goal for this lesson is to experience myself:

The standards I will be using to measure how effectively I control these perceptions are:

In this lesson I will be providing opportunities for students to control what variable?

To what extent do students already perceive this variable?

Are students able to remember this variable?   **YES**   **NO**

What evidence is there for this?

Is there a reference state of this variable?   **YES**   **NO**
What is it?

This form is featured on pages 100-101

What opportunities will I provide students to experience this reference state?

_____
_____
_____

Are the students able to compare the reference state to other states of this variable? **YES   NO**

What opportunities will I provide for students to make these comparisons?

_____
_____
_____
_____
_____

Are the students able to make the necessary adjustments to ensure what they perceive is kept in its reference state? **YES   NO**

What opportunities will I provide for students to make these adjustments?

_____
_____
_____

How much grooving have students been able to do to practice keeping this variable in its reference state?

      a little   some   a lot

What grooving opportunities will I provide for students to practice keeping this variable in its reference state under different conditions?

_____
_____
_____

What information did I obtain from this learning opportunity that I will use to help me plan subsequent opportunities?

_____
_____
_____

Fitting PCAs Into the Network – Whys

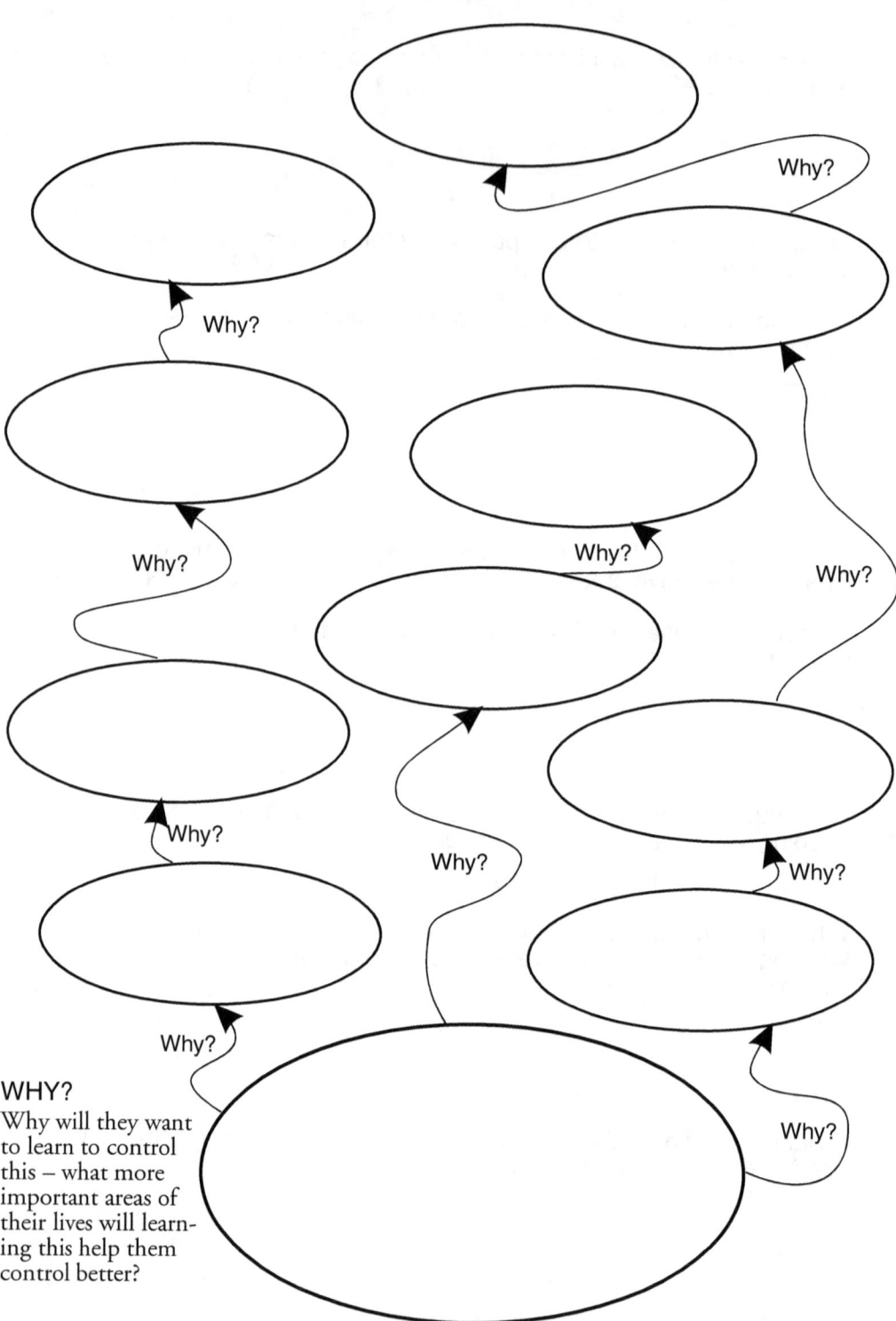

WHY?
Why will they want to learn to control this – what more important areas of their lives will learning this help them control better?

These forms are featured on pages 102-109

Fitting PCAs Into the Network – Hows

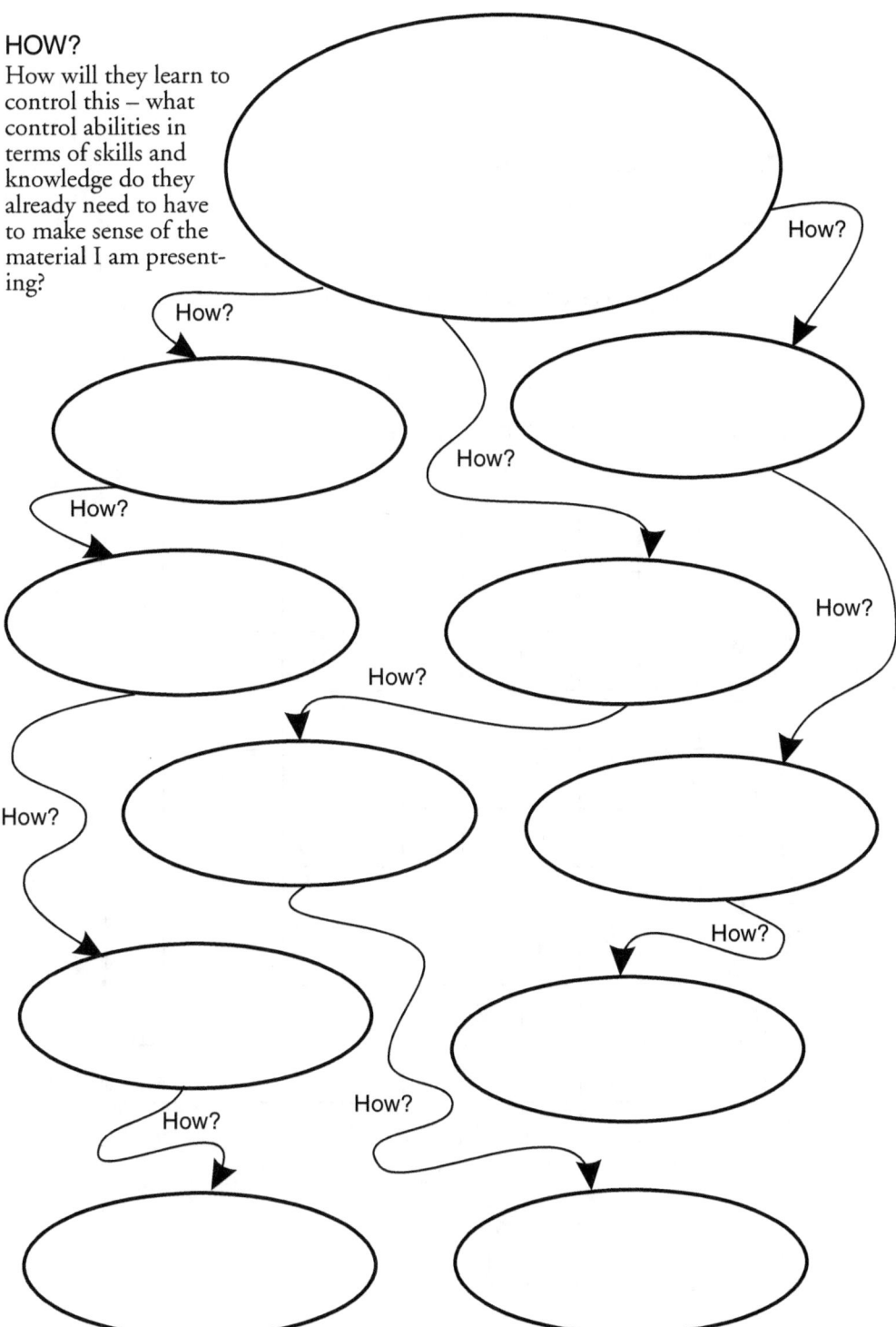

HOW?
How will they learn to control this – what control abilities in terms of skills and knowledge do they already need to have to make sense of the material I am presenting?

Term Planning Sheet

My goal for this term is:

Achieving this goal is important to me because:

To know that I have achieved this goal I will need to:

How close am I to achieving my goal?

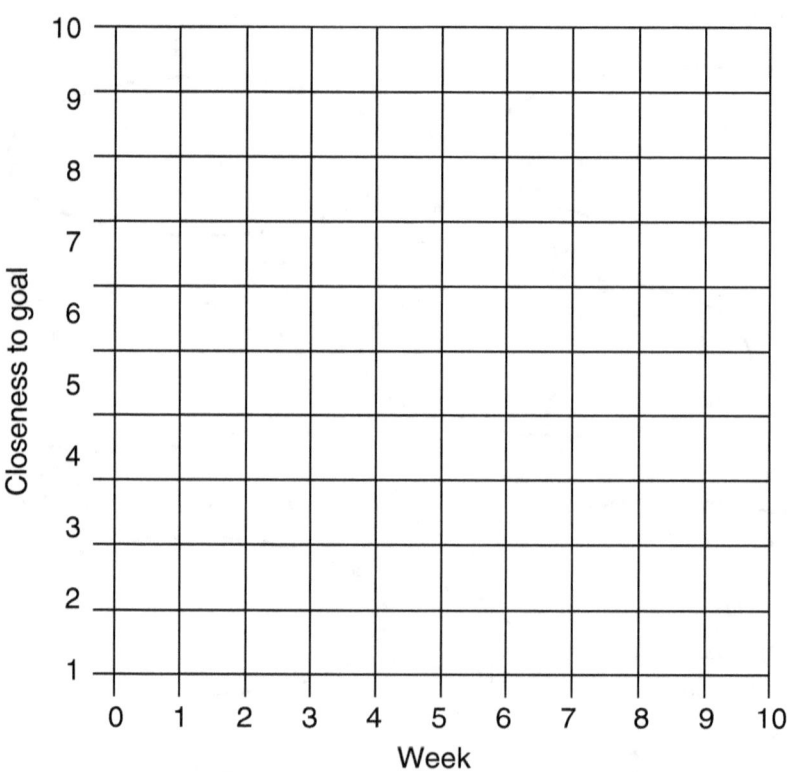

These forms are featured on pages 132-133

Weekly Planning Sheet

My goal for this week:

It will help me achieve my term goal because:

I will get more of what I want in class if I achieve this goal because:

I will know I'm achieving my goal when:

Monday
    need to improve   OK   doing great
    1   2   3   4   5   6   7   8   9   10

Tuesday
    need to improve   OK   doing great
    1   2   3   4   5   6   7   8   9   10

Wednesday
    need to improve   OK   doing great
    1   2   3   4   5   6   7   8   9   10

Thursday
    need to improve   OK   doing great
    1   2   3   4   5   6   7   8   9   10

Friday
    need to improve   OK   doing great
    1   2   3   4   5   6   7   8   9   10

My goal for next week is:

www.ingramcontent.com/pod-product-compliance
Lightning Source LLC
LaVergne TN
LVHW021117080426
835512LV00011B/2548